THE NEW PERSPECTIVE
ON PAUL

THE NEW PERSPECTIVE
ON PAUL

An Introduction

Kent L. Yinger

CASCADE *Books* · Eugene, Oregon

THE NEW PERSPECTIVE ON PAUL
An Introduction

Cascade Books
An Imprint of Wipf and Stock Publishers
199 W. 8th Ave., Suite 3
Eugene, OR 97401

www.wipfandstock.com

ISBN 13: 978-1-60899-463-2

Cataloging-in-Publication data:

Yinger, Kent L.

The new perspective on Paul : an introduction / Kent L. Yinger; with Afterwords by Donald A. Hagner and Don Garlington.

x + 120 p. ; 23 cm. — Includes bibliographical references and index.

ISBN 13: 978-1-60899-463-2

1. Paul, the Apostle, Saint. 2. Bible. N.T. Epistles of Paul—Theology. I. Hagner, Donald Alfred. II. Garlington, Don B. III. Title.

BS2651 Y5 2011

Manufactured in the U.S.A.

To Debi

whose readiness to listen and challenge
has been such an important part of my
own growth in understanding Paul.

CONTENTS

The Conversation Continues
Afterword by Donald A. Hagner / 95
Afterword by Don Garlington / 101

ACKNOWLEDGMENTS

THIS BOOK began to take shape as I was taking up the game of golf again. Between "nice shot" and "now that was a real slice," my regular golf buddies (Geoff, Dave, John and Mike) challenged me to make things understandable (and relatively brief, please). Our church community group deserves thanks for pushing me in the same direction. And long before that, it was Andrew Lincoln's seminary course on Paul and his letters, as well as his later doctoral mentoring, which awakened in me the desire to try and understand this complex man we know as the apostle Paul. George Fox University paved the way for research and writing through numerous leaves and a sabbatical (2008–2009), and my faculty colleagues at George Fox Evangelical Seminary were invaluable discussion partners in writing workshops, faculty research forums, and hallway chats. Special thanks to Rodney Duke and Don Garlington for reading and critiquing an earlier version of this manuscript, to Don Hagner and Don Garlington for agreeing to continue the conversation in writing, and to Wipf and Stock Publishers, and editor Chris Spinks and staff for seeing this project through without delay.

1

WHAT YOU MIGHT OR MIGHT NOT HEAR ABOUT THE "NEW PERSPECTIVE ON PAUL"

"Hey, how was your break?" asks one seminary student of a neighbor. The classroom hums with anticipation on this first day of the semester as my course on Paul is about to begin. Furtively, a new student approaches and in a lowered voice comments, "Good morning, Professor. I'm not sure how to put this, but my pastor wanted me to find out if this class takes a 'New Perspective' approach, or if it sticks to the church's gospel of faith alone? I'm not really sure, myself, what that's all about, but he seemed pretty concerned." Before I can formulate a response, another student, who had been standing behind the questioner, blurts out in excitement, "Oh man, tell your pastor to lighten up; this 'New Perspective' stuff is great. We've got a group of twenty-somethings in our living room once a week, not all Christ-followers, and they're eating it up. A lot of them were turned off to the traditional Paul, anti-woman, anti-Jewish, anti-culture, but they've decided this rediscovered Paul is cool."

Maybe you find yourself in or around one of these attitudes. As we'll see, church leaders and teachers vary widely, some giving dire warnings against and others finding deeper understanding through this New Perspective on Paul. If you're like most I've run across in church and classroom, some basic questions remain unanswered.

- What is it?
- Where did it come from?
- What are the potential dangers?
- What good is it?

This little book aims to answer those questions in understandable language. You shouldn't need a theology degree to read it profitably, but pastors and theology students should find help in getting behind the hype to the real issues. A suggested reading list provides helps for further reading if you want to dig further.

This book will explain the New Perspective on Paul (NPP from here on out) for those less familiar with such debates among scholars. Pulpit and pew are usually thought to be about fifty years behind the progress of Bible scholars. Sometimes this is a good thing; it avoids faddish movements. But other times this is a shame, since it blocks out a better understanding of Scripture. This book hopes to help navigate between faddish innovation and further insight.

The New Perspective on Paul: An Introduction does not engage in overly detailed analysis of the arguments of the NPP. Thus, you might find yourself asking, "But what about [passage X] in Paul's letters?"[1] You'll find concise treatment of a number of such representative passages, but for this detailed analysis of all relevant Bible passages and topics, readers should consult the works listed in the "Suggestions for Further Study" as well as commentaries by supporters and opponents of the NPP.

Neither is this book a defense or critique of the NPP. I have tried to make readers aware of the substantive issues raised by critics as well as the responses of supporters; but for detailed critique and response you will need to consult the works listed in the "Suggestions for Further Study." This list carries brief annotations to help you navigate the literature. My own leanings are pro-NPP. Detractors will undoubtedly think I'm too soft on the NPP. But I also hope proponents will think now and again, "You could have scored a bigger point on that one for our side." I hope both will be able to admit, "That's a pretty fair presentation of my position." Instead of polemic, my desire is that this book be a place where all who genuinely seek to better understand Paul's thought, the central message of this Jewish apostle of Jesus Christ to the Gentiles, can gather and reason together.

---

1. Bible scholars usually make a difference between Paul's seven "undisputed" letters (Romans, 1–2 Corinthians, Galatians, Philippians, 1 Thessalonians, Philemon), which nearly all agree were authored by Paul, and the other "disputed" letters (2 Thessalonians, Colossians, Ephesians, 1–2 Timothy, Titus), over which there are disagreements. I will use all thirteen letters traditionally viewed as authored by Paul, but will make no point that rests solely or primarily on disputed texts.

Thus, you should find everything you need to answer the four questions above in a knowledgeable and fair-minded fashion. If you want a hearty "yes" or "no," there are plenty already available. What most of us lack is something that steps back a bit from the hype and asks, "What really are the issues here?"

2

WHERE DID THIS ALL BEGIN?
E. P. SANDERS AND A
"NEW PERSPECTIVE ON JUDAISM"

L IKE MOST other things in life, changes in opinions, even
opinions about the Bible and theology, usually begin
with dissatisfaction with the status quo. This was certainly
the case with the NPP. In particular, some Bible scholars
were dissatisfied with the way Judaism in the NT era was
being portrayed. This, by the way, is probably one of the
reasons the NPP is less well known outside of academic
circles. Most non-academics remain more-or-less satisfied
with the status quo on this particular issue. "If it ain't broke,
don't fix it."

"JUDAISM" BEFORE SANDERS

During the nineteenth and twentieth centuries NT scholars had come to rely upon a portrayal of Second Temple

Judaism that could be found in nearly all of the standard reference tools of the day.[1]

> **SECOND TEMPLE JUDAISM**
>
> This phrase refers to Judaism from the end of the Jewish exile (when the Jerusalem temple was rebuilt = the second temple) to the destruction of Herod's temple (AD 70). This used to be called the Intertestamental Period, i.e., between the eras of the Old and New Testaments. The beliefs and practices of Jews during this time, including Judaism of the first century, are called "Second Temple Judaism."

This portrayal ran as follows. Jews of the first century were enmeshed in legalism, whereas Paul believed salvation came by grace through faith.

> The Jew takes it for granted that this condition [for God's acquitting decision] is keeping the Law, the accomplishing of "works" prescribed by the Law. In direct contrast to this view Paul's thesis runs . . . "*by, or from, faith.*"[2]

> Pharisaism is the final result of that conception of religion which makes religion consist in conformity to the Law, and promises God's grace only to the doers of the law. It was the scrupulous adherence to legalistic traditions that created the Pharisaic ethos. . . . In Pharisaism this natural tendency [toward outward formalism] became

1. For a survey of these earlier views, see Moore, "Christian Writers on Judaism," 197–254.

2. Bultmann, *Theology of the New Testament*, 1:279–80.

so strong as to give rise to the modern use of the
name Pharisee to describe a self-righteous for-
malist or hypocrite.[3]

This keeping of the Law was a hard burden from which
Jews longed to be released. The 613 commandments and
prohibitions of the Old Testament were spelled out in op-
pressive detail. For example, how many steps could one take
on a Sabbath before it became "work"? By observing these
commands, Jews could attempt to amass sufficient merits to
outweigh the sins on the other side of the scale. Since human
obedience to commandments was the crucial matter in salvation, Jews were fearful of divine judgment. God remained
essentially remote from sinful humanity, including Jews.

It is not hard to see how the gospel was perceived to
contrast at nearly every point with this religion.

- grace versus works
- the Spirit's enablement versus the Law's hard yoke
- joy versus toil
- confidence versus fear, and
- "God with us" versus a remote deity

Scholars even called the Judaism of this period "late Judaism," meaning it was in serious decline and on its last legs.

TURNING POINT 1977

A few writers raised voices of protest. They pointed out
that rabbinic writings were full of the "joy of the commandments," not so much its burden.[4] Instead of earning

3. Metzger, *The New Testament*, 41.
4. Schechter, *Aspects of Rabbinic Theology*, 149–69.

salvation, "A 'lot in the World to come' . . . is ultimately assured to every Israelite on the ground of the original election of the people by the free grace of God."[5] The need to earn salvation by merit is not Jewish. However, such voices had little impact on students of Paul and the NT.

That impact came with the 1977 publication of E. P. Sanders's *Paul and Palestinian Judaism*. This began a wave of dissatisfaction with the common portrayals of Judaism. Sanders devoted nearly four hundred pages to a careful examination of what Jews themselves thought about getting in and staying in God's favor and salvation. Rather than earning divine favor by their works of obedience to his Law, Jews emphasized God's free election of Israel. They were made members of the elect people of God by grace alone. Salvation was a gift, not something they had to first earn.

> I am the LORD, and I will free you from the burdens of the Egyptians and deliver you from slavery to them. I will redeem you with an outstretched arm and with mighty acts of judgment. I will take you as my people, and I will be your God. You shall know that I am the LORD your God, who has freed you from the burdens of the Egyptians. I will bring you into the land that I swore to give to Abraham, Isaac, and Jacob; I will give it to you for a possession. I am the LORD. (Exod 6:6–8)

Of course, God's Law, what Jews call Torah,[6] played a central role in all of this, and obedience to God's commands

5. Moore, *Judaism*, 2:95.

6. English Bible readers misleadingly think of Torah as "law," that is, as a series of legal enactments, commands. While Torah does contain "laws," the Hebrew Torah is a much broader concept, referring

was, indeed, discussed intensively in Judaism. But these commandments were not onerous entry requirements. Instead, Israel was already "in" via the covenant that God had made with the nation. The Law was God's wise and perfect provision to guide his people on the right path. Rigorous obedience to the commandments was the expected response to God's prior act of saving grace, not an attempt to earn it. Both the nation and individuals within the nation kept the commands *not in order to be redeemed* but *because they had been redeemed or saved* (think exodus from Egypt).[7]

COVENANTAL NOMISM

This intimate connection between covenant and command contrasted markedly with the common portrayals of legalistic Judaism up to that point. Sanders gave the name "covenantal nomism" to this Jewish pattern of religion, since it combined covenant and law (Gk. *nomos*).

> Covenantal nomism is the view that one's place in God's plan is established on the basis of the covenant and that the covenant requires as the proper response of man his obedience to its commandments, while providing means of atonement for transgressions.[8]

---

most centrally to God's teaching or instruction and including not only commands and prohibitions, but equally stories, advice, songs, and testimonies.

7. Actually, Jewish sources spoke more about obtaining the promised inheritance, or the land or life, than "salvation," but I will use the more common Christian terminology.

8. Sanders, *Paul and Palestinian Judaism*, 75.

He stressed the primacy of the covenant (God's gracious election) for "getting in" along with obedience to the Law for "staying in." Crucial here, in contrast to previous portrayals of Jewish theology, was the recognition that "obedience maintains one's position in the covenant, but it does not earn God's grace as such."[9] Sanders summarized covenantal nomism in eight points.[10]

1. God has chosen Israel. [Thus, election, or grace, not meritorious works, is the fundamental datum for salvation in Judaism.]

2. And God has given the law. [Torah is a gift to Israel instructing her in the way of life with which God has already graced her; it is not a burden.]

3. The law implies both God's promise to maintain the election and

4. the requirement to obey. [The maintaining of election does not depend solely on the efforts of Israel, but is enabled by God himself. Nevertheless, the importance of actual obedience may never be toned down.]

5. God rewards obedience and punishes transgression.

6. The law provides for means of atonement, and atonement results in

7. maintenance or re-establishment of the covenantal relationship. [Through repentance and the sacrificial system provisions are in place should Israel sin.]

---

9. Ibid., 420, emphasis removed.
10. Ibid., 422. The bracketed comments are my own.

8. All those who are maintained in the covenant by obedience, atonement and God's mercy belong to the group which will be saved.

Far from being the burdensome, hypocritical, and legalistic religion portrayed in most Christian treatments of first-century Judaism (often called Pharisaism), this was a faith that spurred sentiments of reliance upon God's mercy and confession of human weakness.

> As for me, if I stumble,
> the mercies of God shall be my salvation always;
> and if I fall in the sin of the flesh,
> in the justice of God, which endures eternally,
>   shall my judgment be [. . .]
> he will judge me in the justice of his truth,
> and in his plentiful goodness
> always atone for all my sins;
> in his justice he will cleanse me from the
>   uncleanness of the human being
> and from the sin of the sons of man.
>   (1QS 11:12, 14)[11]

> I give you thanks, Lord,
> because you have taught me your truth,
> you have made me know your wonderful
>   mysteries,
> your kindness with sinful men,
> your bountiful compassion with the depraved of
>   heart. (1QH 15:26–27)

For those of us reared on sermons about "self-righteous Pharisees," this represents a huge change. I know from per-

---

11. Unless otherwise noted, all translations of the Dead Sea Scrolls are taken from Martinez, *The Dead Sea Scrolls Translated*.

sonal experience, it takes some time and a fair amount of reflection to digest what this very different view of Judaism means for our understanding of Paul. (More on that in the next chapter.) But, should we swallow *Paul and Palestinian Judaism*? Was Sanders right about this kinder, gentler Judaism? (Sanders's view of Paul is another matter and will occupy a later chapter.) Scholars continue to debate some of the details, but since 1977 general agreement has been reached on the following points:

- First-century Judaism was not the legalistic religion of past caricatures.
- Covenantal nomism is a fair description of Jewish soteriology of the period.[12]

THE DIFFERENCE THIS MAKES

You might be wondering why a book about Paul is talking so much about Judaism. "Why should a new perspective on Judaism make a difference in how we, especially Protestants, understand Paul?" One of the central building blocks of Protestant soteriology is salvation by grace not by works. This discovery of the unmerited grace of God in Jesus Christ has been seen as one of the great advances of the Christian gospel over Judaism. The gospel of free grace has replaced Judaism's hard yoke of keeping the Law, its supposed typical legalism. A few examples will make clear just how much the Protestant interpretation of salvation is indebted to this pre-Sanders view of Judaism.

12. For more detail on post-Sanders debate, see Yinger, "Continuing Quest," 375–91.

In the parable of the Pharisee and the tax collector (Luke 18:9–14) Jesus seems to draw a contrast between the undeserving publican, a self-confessed sinner who can only cry out for mercy, and the self-righteous Pharisee, who boasts of his religious accomplishments ("I fast twice a week") and trusts in himself. Jesus's message (or the Christian gospel) stands upon undeserved mercy in contrast to Judaism's proud self-reliance.

However, if first-century Judaism was not characterized by this self-righteous boasting in merits, what becomes of our interpretation of this parable? Maybe Jesus picked an atypical Pharisee for this story, leaving most of the Pharisees looking more like Sanders's portrayal. But that's not how parables usually operate. The main elements and characters are drawn from common experience. Otherwise, the surprise in the parable doesn't quite work. It arrests the hearers' attention precisely because they assume that Pharisees were among the righteous ones ("justified") and not the despised tax collectors. No, this Pharisee must be typical of most.

Could it be that our view of this Pharisee needs adjustment? He does not boast in self-achieved goodness, but thanks God that he does not walk in sin (v. 11). If so inclined, one could interpret the references to his fasting and tithing as self-righteousness (v. 12). But if Jews kept the Law as a grateful response to God's saving mercy, maybe the Pharisee only refers to his obedience as confirmation of his gratefulness. "Thank you God for making me one of your righteous ones; see, I am seeking to follow your ways, including your commands to fast and tithe." Also, the opening line of the narrative ("He also told this parable to some who trusted in themselves that they were righteous and regarded others with contempt") may actually reflect Jewish covenantal nomism rather than legalistic self-righteousness. They "were convinced of their own righteousness" (v. 9, NAB), not their own self-achieved righteousness, but their status as God's righteous ones given them through election and obedience.[13] Regardless of the correct interpretation of the parable, Sanders's work demands quite a re-evaluation.

Or how about Jesus's parable of the workers in the vineyard? Those who worked longer thought they should be paid more than those hired at the very end of the work day (Matt 20:1–16). Was this a slap against the supposed earning mentality of Judaism? Or is the parable more about the generous behavior of the landowner than the petty calculations of the laborers? "'Are you envious because I am generous?' So the last will be first, and the first will be last" (vv. 15–16). Again, our view of first-century Judaism will have quite an impact on how we hear this story.

Since this book is about the interpretation of Paul, our last example comes from his letters. More clearly than any other author, he speaks of salvation by grace through faith apart from works. "We know that a person is justified not by the works of the law but through faith in Jesus Christ" (Gal 2:16). Traditionally, "justified by the works of the law" points to Jewish legalism. But if Judaism was not particularly legalistic, what in the world is Paul talking about?

If, in fact, Jewish theology of the first century was not particularly legalistic, we're going to have to re-read these and other central passages, and possibly re-envision the Christian understanding of salvation.

13. For more along this line of interpretation, see Holmgren, "The Pharisee and the Tax Collector," 252–61.

- If the Pharisees were not self-righteous legalists, what were they like and why does Jesus contrast the publican with a Pharisee?
- If Judaism did not have an earning mentality, what was the point of the parable of the workers in the vineyard? If not grace versus works, then what?
- And if Jews did not teach salvation by works but salvation by grace, what was Paul so worked up about?

These are no small matters. If the gospel is not fundamentally about grace (Christian) versus works (Judaism), what is it about? Did Jesus and Paul simply misrepresent other Jews—calling them "legalists" when they weren't? And what about all the commentaries, books, and sermons that have helped us understand the gospel by contrasting it with Jewish legalism and pharisaic self-righteousness? Were they wrong?

As we'll see, most proponents of the NPP are not out to overturn the Reformation. Nevertheless, you can now see why the understanding of first-century Judaism makes a huge difference in the understanding of Paul and the Christian gospel, and why the NPP might be a big deal. So, next time you read about the "legalism of the Jews" or hear a message referring to Pharisees trying to earn salvation by their works, a red flag ought to pop up.

3

KICKING OFF THE NEW
PERSPECTIVE ON PAUL
JAMES D. G. DUNN

ALTHOUGH SANDERS'S 1977 volume gave some attention to the interpretation of Paul (actually only about 25% of the book), a lecture by James D. G. Dunn in 1982 marks for most the beginning of what is now known as the New Perspective on Paul.[1] Dunn acknowledged the pivotal role of *Paul and Palestinian Judaism* in shaping his thinking, saying this is the only work of the past couple of decades which "breaks the mould" and demands a major rethinking of Pauline theology. Instead of interpreting Paul's thought as the antithesis of legalistic Judaism (the more traditional approach), we can now interpret him within his

1. The lecture was first published as "The New Perspective on Paul" (1983) and later reprinted with updates in Dunn, *Jesus, Paul, and the Law,* 183–214, and idem, *The New Perspective on Paul,* 99–120.

authentic Jewish context as a Christian apostle who was, and who remained throughout his missionary career, a Jewish theologian.

A MORE JEWISH-SOUNDING PAUL

However, according to Dunn, Sanders had failed to see the continuity between Paul and Judaism. According to Sanders, Paul found a completely new pattern of religion in Christ. Salvation no longer had anything to do with the Jewish covenant but with incorporation into Christ. For Dunn, Sanders's Paul was too disconnected from his Jewish roots, too idiosyncratic. Besides, as Morna Hooker had suggested, covenantal nomism doesn't really sound all that far off from Paul's view of salvation. Both Paul and Judaism (and the Protestant reformers no less) think one gets in by grace and must continue in obedience to reach the final goal.[2]

> Judaism is first and foremost a religion of grace with human obedience always understood as response to that grace. . . . Somewhat surprisingly, the picture which Sanders painted of what he called "covenantal nomism" is remarkably like the classic Reformation theology of works—that good works are the consequence and outworking of divine grace, not the means by which that grace is first attained. . . . The Judaism of what Sanders christened as "covenantal nomism" can now be seen to preach good Protestant doctrine: that grace is always prior; that human effort is ever the response to divine initiative; that good works are the fruit and not the root of salvation.[3]

2. Hooker, "Paul and 'Covenantal Nomism,'" 47–56.
3. Dunn, "The Justice of God," 7–8.

Dunn criticized Sanders for too quickly abandoning the exploration of Paul's relation to his Jewish covenantal nomism in favor of a simple switch of religious patterns.

"BY FAITH NOT WORKS" ACCORDING TO DUNN

Thus, Dunn's NPP attempts to interpret Paul's theology in more continuity with his Jewish covenantal roots. As a prime example, he explores Gal 2:16.

> Yet we know that a person is justified not by the works of the law but through faith in Jesus Christ. And we have come to believe in Christ Jesus, so that we might be justified by faith in Christ, and not by doing the works of the law, because no one will be justified by the works of the law.

Traditionally, the language of "justified not by works but through faith" would point to the stark discontinuity between Paul's new understanding in Christ and his old Jewish views—faith versus works, believing versus doing. Dunn notes, however, that "not by works but through faith" in Gal 2:16 refers to convictions that Paul and other Christian Jews *shared* (like Peter and the Judaizing opponents in Antioch; see vv. 11–15), not views upon which they differed. "We who are Jews by nature and not Gentile sinners, know that a man is not justified by works of law except through faith in Christ Jesus" (Gal 2:15–16, Dunn's translation).[4] Justification is a Jewish covenantal category referring to "God's recognition of Israel as his people, his verdict in favour of Israel on grounds of his covenant with

---

4. For details, see Dunn, *Jesus, Paul, and the Law,* 189–200.

Israel."[5] It is God's marking out of those who are "Jews by birth" from non-Jews, that is, from "Gentile sinners." Unlike Sanders and traditional Pauline interpretation, which see justification by faith as a distinctly Pauline and un-Jewish conviction, Dunn thinks Paul and his Christian Jewish opponents would have agreed on this issue.

"WORKS OF THE LAW"

Where they would disagree is over the role of "works of law." Prior to Sanders, this referred to Jewish legalism, doing works in order to be saved. Dunn argues that this phrase refers not to works-righteousness but to particular observances of the Law that functioned as badges of Jewish identity in the ancient world. In the Antioch incident, where Paul had to confront Peter (Gal 2:11–15), food laws were at issue (see esp. v. 12, "he used to eat with the Gentiles"). Elsewhere in Galatians circumcision plays a central role. Along with Sabbath keeping, these were the practices, the "works of law," that most characteristically identified one as being a member of the covenant people of Israel. Rather than being a code-phrase for legalism, "works of law" could be more accurately understood as a sociological category. It refers to a group of people, the Jewish people, who can be identified by their practice of these "works of law."

NOTE ON ENGLISH TRANSLATIONS OF "WORKS OF LAW"
Readers of English Bibles need to be aware that the translation they read may predetermine for them a particular understanding of "works of law." Paul speaks

5. Ibid., 190.

in Gal 2:16 of being justified *ex ergōn nomou* which could be somewhat neutrally rendered "out of [or from or by] works of law." This is how quite a few translations leave the phrase (NRSV [first half of verse]; KJV; NAB; NASB; ESV). A number of translations, however, take this as a reference to what humans *do* to be justified.

"justified *by doing* the works of the law" (NRSV; second half of verse)

"justified *by observing* the law" (NIV)

"justified *by obeying* the law" (NLT)[6]

The last three English translations lead the reader to assume Paul is speaking of human doing or obeying as the (legalistic) means by which these people are seeking to obtain their own justification. The more neutral translations leave the meaning open to either a NPP or traditional interpretation, depending on how one reads the larger context.

Dunn bolstered his understanding of "works of law" by finding similar usage of the phrase in other Jewish writings. Thus, a number of the Dead Sea Scrolls used the Hebrew equivalent to "works of law" to describe the sect's distinctive practices. By these practices, these "works of law," it became clear who did, and who did not, belong to the sect. The phrase did not suggest a theology of meritorious achievement, but it spoke of how to identify the true followers of God. Paul does the same in Galatians when

6. Eugene Peterson's paraphrase, *The Message*, suggests several legalistic avenues: "by rule-keeping," "by self-improvement," "by trying to be good."

he contrasts those who are "of the works of the law" with "those who are of faith" (Gal 3:9–10).[7]

Thus, when Paul differentiates his position from that of his opponents, he uses the phrase "not by works of law." We might paraphrase this in line with Dunn's understanding as "not by being identified with the Jewish people," or, more simply, "not by being Jewish." Where Paul differed fundamentally from his Jewish tradition was not over the role of grace, faith, and obedience in salvation, but whether salvation was tied to being Jewish or not. In Jewish covenantal nomism, God's election of Israel was fundamental; God's saving work was directed only toward his covenant people. In order to take part in this salvation one needed to be a member of this people. This is what Paul's opponents in Galatia were demanding, that uncircumcised Gentile converts join the covenant people by circumcision. They "try to compel you to be circumcised" (Gal 6:12). After all, they might well have argued, God himself said this identity mark was eternal.

> This is my covenant, which you shall keep, between me and you and your offspring after you: Every male among you shall be circumcised. . . . So shall my covenant be in your flesh an everlasting covenant. (Gen 17:10, 13)

7. This bears similarity to the way he identifies groups in 1 Cor 1:12: "I am of Paul; I am of Peter," etc. To be "of" someone or something is another way of saying "I belong to this group." Thus, "works of law" could simply be the way one group is identified, and Paul is saying that justification no longer comes by identification with the Torah-party, but with Christ.

But Paul remains adamant on this point. Being justified, being reckoned a member of God's saved people, is no longer tied to being Jewish. In fact, he says, "if you let yourselves be circumcised, Christ will be of no benefit to you" (Gal 5:2). Since the coming of Christ the only identity marker of those who belong to God's people is "faith in Christ." As he puts matters, "even we" who are already part of the Jewish covenant people "have come to believe in Christ Jesus, so that we might be justified by faith in Christ, and not by works of the law, because no one will be justified by the works of the law" (Gal 2:16).

Although this crucial phrase, "works of law," appears infrequently in Paul's letters (eight times), its significance lies behind many occurrences of "law" or "works" by themselves, as a kind of short-hand for the fuller phrase. So, for instance, when Paul speaks of "justification through the law" (Gal 2:21) or "by the law" (3:11), he envisions not the individual's effort to merit salvation by keeping the Law, but the Jewish conviction that membership in God's people belongs only to those identified with Torah; this salvation or justification is only "through the (works of) law."

WHAT'S THE CENTRAL QUESTION?

Thus, the primary question being answered in these Pauline texts is not Martin Luther's anguished "How may I, a sinner, find a gracious God?" but "Who belongs to the company of the righteous, to God's saved people?"[8] To read Paul as though he were answering the question, "What must I do to

8. Krister Stendahl pointed out this distinction between Luther's introspective conscience and Paul's more corporate interests in Stendahl, "Introspective Conscience," 78–96.

be saved?" is to misread the apostle's main intent. Instead, those parts of his letters that deal with salvation or justification are usually answering the question, "How may Gentiles take part in God's saving grace to Israel?" It might help to simply read one passage and juxtapose it against these two differing questions.

> Then what becomes of boasting? It is excluded. By what law? By that of works? No, but by the law of faith. For we hold that a person is justified by faith apart from works prescribed by the law. Or is God the God of Jews only? Is he not the God of Gentiles also? Yes, of Gentiles also, since God is one; and he will justify the circumcised on the ground of faith and the uncircumcised through that same faith. (Rom 3:27–30)

A traditional interpretation reads "boasting" as boasting in one's own obedience according to a law, or principle of works; it is self-righteous boasting. Faith excludes such boasting since believing is contrasted with doing (faith versus works); one who simply believes is justified, wholly apart from any doing ("apart from works"), and, thus, no such boasting is possible. This applies equally to Jews and Gentiles since both are to be justified by believing and not by doing.

A NPP reading takes this "boasting" as boasting in Jewish covenantal privilege. Such boasting is ruled out by the "law of faith," that is, by the new identifying mark of faith in Jesus as Messiah. This opening of salvation to non-Jews without becoming Jewish is precisely why Paul immediately says that God is no longer "of Jews only."

So much for Dunn's launching of this NPP in the early 1980s. Since then he has remained one of its most prolific and recognizable proponents.[9] He is by no means, however, the only well-known advocate, nor is his position the only NPP. As we will see in the next chapter there are, in fact, numerous New Perspectives on Paul.

9. For an updated expression of his position, including interaction with critics, see Dunn, "The New Perspective on Paul: Whence, What and Whither?" 1–97.

4

THE NPP SPREADS AND MUTATES
VARIED FORMS OF THE NPP

N. T. WRIGHT

ALTHOUGH STUDENTS of the NPP rightly point to the work of James Dunn for its launch, Anglican bishop and NT scholar N. T. Wright has been a major force in its spread. In fact, he appears to have used the phrase even before Dunn in a 1978 article, in which he offered "a new way of looking at Paul which provides . . . *a new perspective* on other related Pauline problems."[1] Wright's work constitutes a chief expression of the NPP. One of the characteristics of his position is how he sets Paul's theology within the larger biblical story (narrative) of God's work with Israel.

1. Wright, "The Paul of History and the Apostle of Faith," 64 (emphasis added). For a recent statement of Wright's position, see Wright, "Redemption from the New Perspective?"

God's intention for humanity and creation was temporarily derailed through Adam's sin (Gen 1–11). The resolution of this dilemma was the family of Abraham, Israel, through whom the divine blessing was to extend to all humanity (Gen 12). However, the Jewish people failed as well to fulfill their role as the instrument of God's blessing to the world. Instead of being the light for the nations, they wandered from their covenant obligations, ultimately into exile. It would, thus, be left up to Israel's representative to fulfill Adam's originally intended role under God. Messiah Jesus is Israel, the seed of Abraham, the son of God, and his obedience, death, and resurrection are Israel's obedience, death, and resurrection. He is the climax of God's covenantal dealings with Israel and humanity (Adam). Notice, for Wright the story is less about sinful individuals being rescued from judgment for guilt (although it is, for him, also about that),[2] and more about God's fulfillment of his purposes for all creation through Israel.

The mention of exile above brings up another characteristic of Wright's NPP. Sanders thought Paul had first discovered Christ, and then had to figure out what the problem was from which Israel needed saving. As Sanders put matters, Paul's thought moved from solution to plight. Wright argues that Paul, along with other Jews of the period, knew quite well of a plight from which Israel needed deliverance. That plight was the deuteronomic curse of exile in consequence of national disobedience.

2. "To the extent that this sorry state [Israel's exilic condition] included the present sinfulness of Jews as individuals, the normal 'Lutheran' reading can be contained within this analysis" (Wright, *The Climax of the Covenant*, 261).

> And just as the LORD took delight in making
> you prosperous and numerous, so the LORD will
> take delight in bringing you to ruin and destruc-
> tion; you shall be plucked off the land that you
> are entering to possess. The LORD will scatter
> you among all peoples, from one end of the earth
> to the other; and there you shall serve other gods,
> of wood and stone, which neither you nor your
> ancestors have known. (Deut 28:63–64)

Of course, not all Jews of the first century were in literal exile in foreign lands. However, not even those in Judea, Galilee, and Samaria "possessed the land" as promised to Abraham's descendants. The Roman occupation was a daily reminder that Israel had broken the covenant and still awaited the fulfillment of the promises.

But in what way had the nation broken God's covenant? Israel's failure was not "legalism" or "works-righteousness," but "national righteousness, . . . the belief that fleshly Jewish descent guarantees membership of God's true covenant people."[3] Elsewhere Wright terms this a "charter of national privilege." Rather than fulfilling her vocation as a light to the nations, Israel viewed herself in exclusive possession of God's blessings; and only those who became a member of Israel (signified for males by circumcision) could have access to these same blessings. (This corresponds to Dunn's take on "works of law.") However, as John the Baptist had already stated to the nation,

> Do not presume to say to yourselves, "We have
> Abraham as our ancestor"; for I tell you, God
> is able from these stones to raise up children to

---

3. Wright, "The Paul of History and the Apostle of Faith," 65.

> Abraham. Even now the ax is lying at the root of
> the trees; every tree therefore that does not bear
> good fruit is cut down and thrown into the fire.
> (Matt 3:9–10)

NPP: THE MAIN LINES

Thus, Wright and Dunn have laid down the main lines of
what has become known as the NPP, sometimes simply referred to as the (Sanders-)Dunn-Wright-trajectory. Students
should know that these two scholars do not agree on everything regarding Paul and Judaism. For instance, Dunn
is more cautious than Wright regarding the use of story or
narrative,[4] and Wright disagrees with details of Dunn's exegesis of Gal 3:10–14.[5] Nevertheless, the main lines of the
NPP should be clear enough.[6]

1. First-century Judaisms were not legalistic, but were
   characterized by covenantal nomism—saved by God's
   grace and obligated to follow his ways.

2. Since Jews were not espousing works-righteousness,
   Paul was not opposing legalism in his letters.

3. Instead, at issue was a question of social identity: "Who
   belongs to the people of God and how is this known?"
   i.e., does one have to be Jewish—be circumcised, keep

---

4. Dunn, "Narrative Approach to Paul," 217–30.

5. "Tortuous and improbable," Wright, *The Climax of the Covenant*,
153.

6. Points one to three correspond largely to Westerholm's summary of the NPP: Westerholm, *Perspectives Old and New on Paul*,
249–58. See also the recent summary in Dunn, *The New Perspective
on Paul Revised Edition*, 16–17.

food laws, celebrate Sabbath, etc.—in order to inherit the promises to Abraham?

4. Paul does not differ from most other Jews as to the roles of grace, faith, and works in salvation; where he differs is the conviction that Jesus is Israel's Messiah and the Lord of all creation. No longer is Torah the defining center of God's dealings; what counts now is belonging to Christ.[7]

ADDITIONAL DEFENDERS

Some subsequent writers have adopted this interpretive framework and refined various aspects. Don Garlington, for instance, has explored the importance of Paul's phrase, "the obedience of faith" (Rom 1:5; 16:26). His work highlights the eschatological, or already/not-yet nature of justification. Believers are already justified by grace through faith in Christ. Yet, they still await final justification (or vindication, deliverance from final wrath). This makes sense, according to Garlington, once we see that all of Christ's benefits are available only "in Christ," that is, via union with Christ. Thus, for Paul it is necessary not only to begin the journey of faith in Christ, but equally to persevere in "the obedience of faith" to the end, that is, to remain "in Christ."[8]

My own work also falls clearly within the NPP camp. In particular, *Paul, Judaism and Judgment According to Deeds* attempts to demonstrate that Paul did not break with his Jewish convictions regarding the role of works, or obedience, in final salvation. His insistence that Christ-believers would

---

7. For this last point, see ch. 3 above, "Works of Law," pages 20–23.

8. Garlington, *The Obedience of Faith.*

be judged according to their deeds (for salvation) reiterates both the language and the concepts he had earlier learned.

> For all of us must appear before the judgment seat of Christ, so that each may receive recompense for what has been done in the body, whether good or evil. (2 Cor 5:10)

NEW PERSPECTIVES: MORE THAN ONE?

One of the more confusing realities for students wading into this field of study is the diversity of New Perspectives on Paul. Yes, "perspectives"—plural. Hardly any single author is the clone of another. Thus, scholars refer to the "*so-called* New Perspective on Paul" in order to emphasize that there really is no single authoritative position. As N. T. Wright himself noted in 2003, "there are probably almost as many 'New Perspective' positions as there are writers espousing it—and . . . I disagree with most of them."[9] What follows is hardly a comprehensive survey of all the variations, but I will attempt to introduce you to a number of the major developments. Keep in mind, not all of these would themselves be equally happy to accept the label NPP.

SOCIAL INTERPRETATION

The importance of social identity is already clear from the work of Dunn and Wright; "works of law" has as much to do with one's social location (membership in the covenant group) as it does with theology. Some authors contend that such social realities were far more significant to Paul and

9. See Wright, "New Perspectives on Paul."

may, in fact, eclipse the importance of theological concerns for the apostle. According to Francis Watson, Paul was far more interested in establishing and defending his new Gentile communities of faith than in debating points of theology. In fact, the theological debates were only carried out for pragmatic reasons, i.e., as a way to legitimize his new communities in the eyes of others.

> Paul's sole aim in discussing Judaism and the law is to maintain and defend the separation of the Gentile Christian churches from the Jewish community. In fulfilling this aim, he makes use of various types of theoretical legitimation, which are not always compatible with one another as pure theory, but which all contribute to the same practical goal.[10]

Watson calls for the abandonment of an overtly theological approach characteristic of the Reformation. The attempt to produce a harmonious Pauline theology will prove difficult, if not impossible, since the apostle marshals his theological arguments on the run, so to speak, to lend weight to his greater concern—the preservation of his communities.

A Non-Systematic Paul

This last sentence leads nicely into another development— the inconsistent, or even incoherent, Paul. Like most NPP proponents, the Finnish Lutheran Heikki Räisänen builds upon covenantal nomism as an adequate description of Jewish soteriology in the first century and seeks to understand Paul in its light.[11] However, whereas traditional

10. Watson, *Paul, Judaism, and the Gentiles,* 22.

11. Räisänen, *Paul and the Law.*

interpretation stresses discontinuity (Pauline grace versus Jewish legalism) and other NPP writers point out continuity, Räisänen calls into question the assumption on both sides that Paul was a systematic or coherent thinker. In point of fact, argues Räisänen, Paul's attitude toward the Jewish Law vacillates between positive and negative throughout his letters. It can be an enslaving power from which we need freedom ("a yoke of slavery," Gal 5:1) and a good and spiritual reality (Rom 7:12, 14). Its validity has come to an end (Rom 10:4), yet Christians are still called to fulfill it (Rom 13:8–10). The reason for this inner contradiction is simple. "We find Paul struggling with the problem that a divine institution has been abolished through what God has done in Christ."[12]

AN ANTI-IMPERIAL PAUL

Although not originally connected with NPP developments, another approach to interpreting Paul's letters has overlapped to some degree and influenced certain NPP presentations. This is anti-imperial interpretation. Jesus's message of God as present and coming king ("kingdom of God"), as well as Paul's message of Jesus as Lord, were primarily aimed against Roman imperial ideology. Caesar was not king; God was. The emperor was not lord and savior of all; Jesus was.[13] While N. T. Wright has certainly not repudiated his earlier NPP stance, he now prefers a broader approach, a "fresh

12. Ibid., 264–65

13. Again, students need caution not to lump all anti-imperial interpreters into the NPP camp. When Horsley states, "Paul's gospel opposed the Roman imperial order, not Judaism," he moves in a different direction ("Introduction," 3).

perspective," which incorporates this anti-imperial note.[14] Paul's concerns were not only with God's work in and for Israel, but more deeply with God's work in the empire of Rome and in the entire creation. The God of the Bible is up to more than simply saving individuals or a people (although he is also out to do that), he is out to reclaim his rule over this world and cosmos.

TWO COVENANTS

Another development sometimes associated with the NPP involves variations of two-covenant soteriology.[15] One of the concerns driving Sanders's work on Judaism was an anti-Jewish bias arising from many traditional portrayals of legalistic Judaism. In Sanders's work, Jewish covenantal nomism comes off so well, one wonders why anyone would find fault with it. As Sanders himself put matters, there really was no "plight" from which Paul felt he needed to be rescued as a Jew. Paul's gospel arose not so much from opposition to Judaism, but was a new parallel track or pattern of religion. Along these same lines, a number of scholars have suggested that Paul's gospel targeted Gentiles, not Jews. The Jewish way of Torah-observance remained, even in Paul's thinking, quite adequate for Jews. "Circumcision indeed is of value if you obey the law" (Rom 2:25). It was

14. Wright, *Paul: In Fresh Perspective*; see esp. chap. 4, "Gospel and Empire."

15. See especially Gager, *Origins*, and Gaston, *Paul and the Torah*. Although Stendahl's early work seemed to lead in this direction, he has distanced himself, preferring to leave the question of Paul and the salvation of the Jews to the realm of mystery; Stendahl, *Final Account: Paul's Letter to the Romans*.

inadequate only when applied to Gentiles. For them Christ had opened a new Torah-free way through faith without circumcision. Thus, there are two saving covenants in operation since Christ—the Torah covenant for Jews, and the Christ covenant for Gentiles. Both Dunn and Wright resist this conclusion.

Moving Beyond the NPP

The last development to mention relates to the many now calling for us to move beyond the NPP. Some of these want to move on because they view the NPP as more-or-less incorrect; it needs to be left behind. These more critical voices will occupy the next chapter. Here I focus on those who think Sanders was more-or-less on target regarding Judaism, and who think that Paul was not opposing legalistic Judaism. However, they have come to feel that this starting point is insufficient for one reason or another. Bruce Longenecker, for instance, thinks that some sort of complementarity, rather than antithesis, between new and traditional perspectives may be the way forward. Instead of the current *either-or* standoff, some sort of *both-and* will prove workable.[16] Similarly, Michael Bird thinks there is a *via media* if only both sides will soften some of their sharper edges.[17] Thus, justification should be seen as *both* social and soteriological, *both* communal and individual, *both* covenantal and forensic. While the idea of the imputed righteousness of Christ may be retained for theological discussion (a nod to traditional interpretation), incorporated

16. Longenecker, "Perspectives on Paul and the Law," 125–30; see also idem, *The Triumph of Abraham's God*, 179–83.

17. Bird, *The Saving Righteousness of God*.

righteousness, or participation in Christ, is more accurate to describe Paul's own position (with the NPP).[18] As with most mediating positions, neither of the sides feels, thus far, that the mediation has quite got their position right.[19]

Hopefully the reader now has a better grasp of the New Perspective on Paul, or, more accurately, the various perspectives that draw some inspiration from the work of E. P. Sanders on Judaism. Of course, neither traditional nor new perspectives cover all of the modern approaches to studying Paul. For some scholars the NPP is already passé. Others find the interpretive key elsewhere.[20] Still others warn of serious dangers in swallowing the NPP (see the following chapters), while another group maintains the continuing promise of this approach (see especially the final chapter).

18. For discussion of some of these technical terms ("justification," "forensic," etc.), see ch. 7 below.

19. Don Hagner thinks such harmonizing will prove impossible; "Paul and Judaism: Testing the New Perspective," in Stuhlmacher, *Revisiting Paul's Doctrine of Justification*, 100n77.

20. For example, Campbell, *The Quest for Paul's Gospel*, stresses apocalyptic discontinuity. That is, the radical newness of what God has done in Christ overpowers any perceived continuity with Paul's Jewish past. "See, everything has become new!" (2 Cor 5:17).

5

THE FUR STARTS FLYING
CONCERNS OVER SANDERS'S JUDAISM

IF YOU'VE followed developments thus far, you might be thinking, "sounds like a rather arcane academic debate to me. Do pastors and church folks really care?" A quick spin on the information superhighway or down the aisles of your local Christian bookstore will make clear, this debate has definitely leaked out beyond the ivory towers. One Web site includes 108 links(!) to online critiques of the NPP.[1] A sermon site reproduces one of Charles Spurgeon's sermons (nineteenth century!) on justification, and comments,

> Spurgeon here defends the classic biblical (Puritan) teaching in such a way that you might think that he was refuting some of the modern attacks on this teaching by . . . teachers of heresy like

1. See monergism.com.

N. T. Wright and the New Perspective on Paul movement.[2]

Churches and their Web sites warn the flock against NPP scholars who "see themselves as the first people since the early Church Fathers who have rightly understood Paul and his message."[3] Barnes & Noble lists sixteen titles under "New Perspective on Paul" (as of July 2009). Of course, the pro-NPP side is certainly not without its Web presence either.[4] Depending on which book or Web page you discover, Paul is either rescued or betrayed by the NPP. Or, if you prefer face-to-face interaction, without doubt there is a conference not too far away with a roster of either supporters or opponents. Some of the major scholarly supporters have been mentioned in previous chapters. The critics also have their heavyweights, including respected scholars, like D. A. Carson of Trinity Evangelical Divinity School, and influential pastors, like John Piper of Bethlehem Baptist in Minneapolis.

My aim in the next three chapters is to alert you to many of the specific debates and concerns raging about the NPP, to let you see in more detail what those charges are, and how NPP writers respond. It is not my aim to engage in these disputes and to try to resolve them; for that you should look to the writers on either side listed in the notes or bibliography. The concerns fall broadly into three categories, the first of which will be the subject of this chapter.

---

2. Comment on "Justification" sermon by Spurgeon.

3. Gilley, "The New Perspective on Paul, Part 1."

4. For a more NPP-friendly site, see www.thepaulpage.com.

- Was Sanders right about the non-legalistic nature of first-century Judaism?
- But what about the Greek word in that verse? That is, concerns about the interpretation of specific verses or passages.
- Concerns about theology, church history, and ministry.

WAS FIRST-CENTURY JUDAISM REALLY SO GRACIOUS AND NON-LEGALISTIC?

If Paul's Jewish antagonists really did think they needed to amass sufficient merit to be saved (legalism), then maybe the entire NPP search for some other non-legalistic target was unnecessary and wrong-headed. If Sanders's new perspective *on Judaism* has serious cracks, so too does the new perspective *on Paul*.

Academic treatments sometimes point to the prolific Jewish scholar Jacob Neusner as an early critic of Sanders's reconstruction of covenantal nomism. Neusner, to be sure, was highly critical of *Paul and Palestinian Judaism*.

> In regard to Rabbinic Judaism, Sanders' book also is so profoundly flawed as to be hopeless and, I regret to say it, useless in accomplishing its stated goals of systemic description and comparison.[5]

However, this negative assessment had to do with the book's methodology, not so much with the description of covenantal nomism. Neusner was perturbed that Sanders had treated Jewish texts as though they were intended to

5. Neusner, "Paul and Palestinian Judaism," 191.

answer Christian theological questions, such as the role of grace, faith, and works in salvation. Neusner objected that most Jewish texts were not particularly concerned with what Christians term "salvation," but were generated by other issues. Neusner, however, was quite content with covenantal nomism.

> So far as Sanders proposes to demonstrate the importance to all the kinds of ancient Judaism of covenantal nomism, election, atonement, and the like, his work must be pronounced a complete success.[6]

Thus, students will be hard-pressed to find more recent scholars seeking to return to a pre-Sanders view (caricature?) of legalistic Judaism.[7] Instead, John Barclay's judgment is representative:

> On the whole, [Sanders's] analysis of the structure of thought in Palestinian Judaism has been widely acknowledged as accurate and convincing.[8]

OTHER KINDS OF JUDAISM?

Even if covenantal nomism is a correct description of most Jewish thought of the period, does it accurately depict all of the many variegated forms? Since not all first-century Jews thought exactly alike, perhaps some were more legalistic than others. A concerted probe in this direction was

6. Ibid., 180.

7. For a more in-depth treatment of these sorts of debates over Judaism, see Yinger, "Continuing Quest."

8. Barclay, "Paul and the Law," 8.

published in 2001.[9] More than a dozen scholars examined a wide variety of Second Temple Jewish literature and found that some texts seem supportive of covenantal nomism, others are silent or unclear on the subject, and a few may evidence some type of legalism. Some skeptics of the NPP have already begun to tout this and similar volumes as another nail in its coffin.

How do NPP proponents respond to this challenge? There is, in point of fact, continued need for more detailed work on the interpretation of quite a number of Second Temple Jewish texts; the study of Judaism did not reach its climax in 1977. Along the same lines, we may indeed find evidence in this or that Jewish text for legalistic convictions.[10] Sanders himself felt one text (4 Ezra) was an exception to his non-legalistic rule. Nor should we be surprised if some Jews failed to keep the proper balance. Every religious tradition produces quite a variety of fruit. However, the discovery of a few aberrant forms of Judaism does not alter our perception of mainstream Jewish soteriology. For such discoveries to make a difference, they would either need to be more widespread, or Paul would need to have been influenced by this side current. The critics have demonstrated neither point.

NPP writers generally do not stress the monolithic nature of first-century Judaism as charged, but are quite willing to acknowledge the diversity within Judaisms of the day. The question, then, becomes, within all this diversity,

9. Carson, O'Brien, Seifrid, eds., *Justification and Variegated Nomism.*

10. Of course, one too often ignored problem is agreeing on what we mean by "legalism." See Yinger, "Defining 'Legalism,'" 91–108.

is there any common core remaining which we might identify as "Judaism"? Was there anything on which most Jews
would have found common cause? NPP writers (along with
a broad array of Jewish, OT, and NT scholars) remain convinced that covenantal nomism still does quite well as a general depiction of Jewish soteriology and of Paul's Judaism.

LEGALISM MAY LURK ELSEWHERE

Another challenge to covenantal nomism finds Jewish legalism elsewhere; namely, in Paul's Christian perspective
on his former Jewish views. That is, granted Jews were not
legalists in their self-understanding, but as Paul looks back
from his new Christian understanding he perceives that
works played (or logically ought to have played) a different
role in Judaism than they now do in his faith in Christ. This
is what Paul means when he says he has now come to regard
what he formerly valued in Judaism as "rubbish" (Phil 3:8).[11]
Thus, this tack turns out to be not so much a challenge to
Sanders's views of Judaism—these writers appear willing
to accept something like covenantal nomism for a description of Jewish self-understanding—as a challenge to certain
NPP interpretations of Pauline concepts and passages. For
instance, they contend that Paul's radically different understanding of grace has changed the way he relates faith and
works. Since this is not really a critique of Sanders's view
of Judaism, but of NPP interpretation of Pauline texts and
theology, such points will occupy the next two chapters.

---

11. A number of recent authors take this approach. See, for example, Das, *Paul and the Jews*; and Gathercole, *Where Is Boasting?*

Seeing the difficulty of proving legalism from Jewish texts, some make an appeal to "a natural human tendency toward legalism."[12] Again, this is hardly a telling criticism of Sanders's work, but reflects theological concerns; namely, the NPP may allow a general human proclivity toward works-righteousness to slip in through the back door. This and other theological critiques will occupy the next chapter.

TOO MUCH "COVENANTAL" NOT ENOUGH "NOMISM"

A final criticism seems to have been taken to heart by some NPP writers. Namely, in highlighting covenantal grace in Jewish soteriology Sanders may have portrayed Judaism's stress on good works in overly soft tones. The covenantal part of covenantal nomism—grace and election—can be made so primary that the nomism element—the necessity to actually do the Law—gets spoken too softly, or is reduced to a mere boundary marker.[13] To the extent that Sanders or NPP writers give the impression that salvation is wholly due to covenantal grace, and that actual, laborious obedience to Torah's demands is somehow toned down or made secondary, the criticism is worth a hearing. In the main, however, the criticism may miss the mark. The whole point of covenantal nomism was to hold together both divine and human agency as equally necessary. The ubiquitous Jewish motif of judgment according to deeds, which Sanders, Dunn and most NPP writers incorporate

12. Hagner, "Paul and Judaism," 119.

13. See, for example, Watson, "Not the New Perspective"; or idem, *Paul, Judaism, and the Gentiles*, 12–21.

into their understanding of covenantal nomism, hardly amounts to an overly soft portrait.[14]

This chapter has examined criticisms of the NPP with which many readers are probably less familiar, since the details of the arguments deal with Jewish texts lying outside a normal Christian readership (1 Enoch, Dead Sea Scrolls, Testament of the Twelve Patriarchs, etc.) and with fine points of Hebrew and Aramaic languages. The next two chapters will tread on more familiar territory, Paul's letters and theology.

14. For this response, see Dunn, *The New Perspective on Paul Revised Edition*, 58–71.

6

EXEGETICAL CONCERNS

THE PROOF of any theory about interpreting Paul's letters lies, of course, in the pudding of exegesis (= method of interpretation). That is, can the theory actually make good sense of what Paul said—and not just some of what the apostle wrote, but all of it? Students need to be aware, again, that there is no single "New Perspective interpretation" of a given passage. NPP authors not infrequently disagree among themselves, just as their critics disagree among themselves. Thus, the best we can do in this chapter is to make readers aware of some typical interpretations on both sides. In this way, readers can obtain a good feel for what difference the NPP might make in reading the NT. The passages chosen for examination are the ones that crop up again and again in the literature, but they are by no means exhaustive of the exegetical concerns of the critics.

WORKS OF LAW

One early concern had to do with Dunn's interpretation of "works of law." He argues that the term referred to Jewish Torah practices which functioned as identity badges in the ancient world. In particular, there were three such identifiers mentioned in the Letter to the Galatians and which were widely utilized by non-Jews to mark out who was or was not a Jew: circumcision, food laws, Sabbath regulations. Critics cried "foul" at this seeming restriction of "works of law" to only these areas of obedience. Surely, they protested, Paul had a broader obedience in mind, including obedience to all that the Law commands. In Gal 3:10 those who are of the works of the Law and under a curse are precisely those who fail to obey "*all* the things written in the book of the law," not simply the three identity markers.

Dunn has since clarified that he actually agrees with his critics on this point. "Works of law" does refer generally to all of those practices commanded by Torah. However, he still maintains, the dispute in the Galatian letter revolves around one specific Torah command, circumcision, by which Gentile converts were being enticed to obtain Jewish identity. This debate turns out to be a bit like a mother trying to get her three-year-old to eat vegetables. Of course, the mother's ultimate desire is that the child eats all her vegetables. At the moment, however, "all vegetables" is focused on the spinach that is on her plate. So in Galatia, "all the works of law" is focused on those marks of Jewish identity that are particularly in dispute.[1]

---

1. For a recent statement of Dunn's position, see Dunn, "The New Perspective on Paul: Whence, What and Whither?" 23–28.

At a deeper level, critics object to this seeming reduction of "works of law" to a sociological issue. Doing these works seems no longer to have much to do with one's salvation, only with whether one belongs to a particular social group or not. Here students must be careful not to lump all NPP writers indiscriminately together. Some do lean so strongly on the side of a sociological approach to interpreting Paul that his theological views become secondary.[2] The views of Dunn and Wright, on the other hand, represent more of a *both-and* to this issue of sociology versus theology. "Works of law" do identify one's social positioning (Jewish, non-Jewish), but precisely this social identity is central to the theological issue of justification. Being part of Abraham's offspring (Gal 3) is both a sociological and theological matter.

Of course, most deeply in dispute is whether or not "works of law" has something to do with legalism. When Paul objects to justification "by works of law" (Gal 2:16), does this refer to the more traditional conviction that doing these works will earn justification (= legalism), or that one must belong to the covenant group, Israel? I will not repeat what has been explored previously on this question (see pages 20–23 above). This exegetical debate seems to have reached an impasse. Again, students need to distinguish exegetical and theological issues here. Whether Paul opposed legalism is a larger issue than the exegesis of one

2. For one example, see Watson, *Paul, Judaism, and the Gentiles.* Though not representative of my own perspective, this attention to sociology should not be flippantly tossed aside. Most of us are far too unaware of just how deeply our theological views are influenced by our upbringing and by the groups and movements with which we identify and find personal meaning.

phrase. Like most Jews of the day, Paul surely thought that legalism—doing enough to put God in our debt so that he "owes" us salvation—was ludicrous, even if that's not what he's talking about with "works of law." Critics fear that the NPP slips in legalism through a side door; NPP writers do not typically approve of legalism, but contend that particular passages in Paul deal with something else. Either way, this is a larger theological concern and will be dealt with in the next chapter.

PAUL: CONVERTED OR CALLED?[3]

Since the NPP builds upon a new perspective on Judaism it is not surprising that Paul's relationship to Judaism, or to the Jewish Law, forms a main bone of contention. In most non-NPP readings of Paul's letters, the apostle glimpses on the road to Damascus the inadequacy of his former Jewish theology, and turns to a new way, faith in Christ. Paul leaves many aspects of his former Jewish identity and becomes a Christian. One surprising question that arises in this regard is, was Paul converted? That is, after the Damascus road experience, did he remain an adherent of Judaism, or did he convert to something else? The question turns out to be not quite as silly as it sounds at first. Of course, on the one hand, a radical change unquestionably happened to Saul, the Pharisee. The persecutor of Christ-followers became himself one of them. If such an about-face regarding Jesus, a change of mind on certain matters, is what we mean by "conversion," then surely Paul was converted.

---

3. The classic pre-NPP expression of this issue is found in Stendahl, "Introspective Conscience," 7–23 ("Call Rather Than Conversion").

But the issue is not quite so simple as that. When someone "converts" or has a "conversion" experience, we typically think of a change of religion. With this understanding of the meaning of conversion, we have Paul leaving his Jewish religion and converting to Christianity. Saul the Pharisee became Paul the apostle of Christ. This kind of radical religious discontinuity can be found throughout older literature about the apostle. The difficulties with putting things this way are manifold and go to the heart of the NPP.

First, to speak of Paul switching religions to Christianity is anachronistic. That is, we are taking a later situation and imposing it on an earlier, quite different, situation. In the middle of the first century there was not yet an identifiable religion called "Christianity." Occasionally Jesus-followers were called *christianoi* (Acts 11:26; 26:28; 1 Pet 4:16), but this was simply the way some antagonists tried to label and differentiate these folks from others as supporters of a particular figure or party, Christ.[4] Paul did not have to quit Judaism to become a Christ-follower.[5]

Second, this use of "conversion" for Paul muddies the water as to one of the main issues in his letters. Paul's gospel, rather than being an attempt to persuade folks to leave (legalistic) Judaism for (gracious) Christianity, is the key in his struggle over the identity of this Christ-movement in the Roman Empire. Although originally a Jewish movement centered in Galilee and Judea, now more and more

4. Thus, supporters of Herod were called *hērōdianoi* (Mark 3:6). The first recorded use of the noun "Christianity" (Gk. *christianismos*) comes around AD 100 by Ignatius of Antioch.

5. Acts 15:5 speaks of some early Jewish Christians ("believers") who simultaneously "belonged to the sect of the Pharisees."

non-Jews, Gentiles, are hopping on board. Some preachers, like Paul, are saying they don't even need to bear the marks of Jewish identity in order to belong to this Jewish movement. They can be justified by faith in Christ rather than by being Jewish ("works of law"). Others are just as adamant that they do need to become Jewish ("it is necessary for them to be circumcised," Acts 15:5). Jews are already in a precarious situation in the empire—exempted from some common civic duties like sacrificing to the gods, but resented by the populace for being granted such exemptions and sometimes oppressed or even persecuted by government officials. If Paul's non-Jewish Christ-followers are considered part of this Jewish Christ-party, the whole precarious arrangement threatens to collapse.

And third, Paul himself uses the language of prophetic calling rather than conversion for this element in his life. "But when God, who had set me apart before I was born and called me through his grace . . ." (Gal 1:15; see also Rom 1:1). Paul seems to consciously echo the language of God's call to prophets like Jeremiah and Isaiah. "Before I formed you in the womb I knew you, and before you were born I consecrated you; I appointed you a prophet to the nations" (Jer 1:5). "The LORD called me before I was born. [. . .] to raise up the tribes of Jacob and to restore the survivors of Israel; I will give you as a light to the nations, that my salvation may reach to the end of the earth" (Isa 49:1, 6). Paul did not view himself as preaching a change of religions, but as a Jewish prophet calling Israel and the nations to follow the God of Israel who has now revealed himself at the end of time in Messiah Jesus.

So, "Was Paul converted?" turns out to be not such a simple or silly question after all.[6] How one answers this question reveals quite a bit about one's assumptions in relation to many issues connected to the NPP. But before moving on, we should take a brief look at one passage that seems to point unmistakably toward Paul's conversion.

> You have heard, no doubt, of my earlier life in Judaism. I was violently persecuting the church of God and was trying to destroy it. I advanced in Judaism beyond many among my people of the same age, for I was far more zealous for the traditions of my ancestors. (Gal 1:13–14)

Surely "my earlier life in Judaism" means that Paul no longer considers himself an adherent of "Judaism," that he converted from the Jewish religion to another faith. Not so fast, object NPP writers. Here again, they argue, we are inserting our modern notion of Judaism as a religion distinct from Christianity into this passage. Instead, use of the noun "Judaism" was quite rare in this period and referred not to the general beliefs and praxis of Jews, but more specifically to forms of Jewishness that defined themselves in opposition to Hellenism. Unlike Jews who compromised with Hellenistic culture, these Jews were zealous for Israel's Law and ancestral traditions, and were prepared to fight— even to die—to maintain Israel's distinctiveness over against Greek, Roman, or even looser Jewish ways. As a Pharisee, Paul, too, "was violently persecuting" those who endangered

6. Those interested in the ongoing debate could read Segal, *Paul the Convert* (a conversion "within" but not "from" Judaism), and Dunn, "Paul's Conversion," 347–65 (NPP); or Barnett, *Paul: Missionary of Jesus*, 54–75 (traditional view, "converted").

Israel's distinctive identity and "was far more zealous for the traditions of my ancestors" than other Jews. Yes, indeed, Paul changed his mind, converted, from this form of Jewish zeal, from this "Judaism," but the passage does not mean he abandoned the beliefs and praxis of Jews generally.[7] Paul stills insists "we ourselves are Jews by birth and not Gentile sinners" (Gal 2:15).

WHAT EXACTLY WAS THE CURSE OF THE LAW?

Galatians 3:10–13 is another passage that crops up repeatedly in debates over the NPP since it appears to highlight something inherently deficient in Judaism and its Law, something that inevitably brings a curse.

> For all who rely on the works of the law [lit. "all who are of works of law" (see pages 20–21 and 21n6 above)] are under a curse; for it is written, "Cursed is everyone who does not observe and obey all the things written in the book of the law." Now it is evident that no one is justified before God by the law; for "The one who is righteous will live by faith." But the law does not rest on faith; on the contrary, "Whoever does the works of the law will live by them." Christ redeemed us from the curse of the law by becoming a curse for us—for it is written, "Cursed is everyone who hangs on a tree." (Gal 3:10–13)

At least since the Reformation it has been common to perceive the following logic at work in this text.

---

7. For this line of argument, see esp. Dunn, "Paul's Conversion," 357–62.

1. The Law pronounces a curse upon anyone who fails to keep it. (Paul quotes Deut 27:26.)

2. No human being can keep the Law perfectly.

3. Thus, all human beings fall under the Law's curse.

4. However, Christ took upon himself humanity's sin and curse at the cross, and thus purchased release from this curse.

The problem is rooted in the Law's demand (perfect obedience, point 2 above) and humanity's sinful inability to deliver such obedience.[8]

NPP writers take issue with this depiction of how Judaism and its Law worked. In particular, they reject the implied premise that the Law required perfect obedience (points 1 and 2 above). Sanders had made this point earlier, as had numerous Jewish scholars. They pointed to the sacrificial system, the possibility of repentance, and divine forgiveness all as allowing for something less than perfect obedience, i.e., as making provision for imperfections.[9]

But if the obedience required by the Law was something less than perfection and quite within human ability under covenantal grace, what is Paul's point in bringing up the curse of the Law? Here there is no uniform NPP answer. Dunn notes that the curse in verse 10 falls not on those who rely on their perfect obedience, but on everyone who is "of works of Law," that is, on everyone who relies on their

8. An advocate of this view is Schreiner, "Is Perfect Obedience to the Law Possible," 151–60. Note, Schreiner does not think that Judaism or the OT taught this, but that Paul now saw this to be the case about Judaism and the Law since coming to Christ.

9. See Cranford, "The Possibility of Perfect Obedience," 242–58.

Jewish covenantal identity for justification. The curse falls upon Israel's nationalistic or ethnocentric righteousness, which wants to tie divine justification exclusively to Jewish identity, thus excluding Gentiles. According to N. T. Wright, the curse refers to the consequences of Israel's national disobedience, and especially to the curse of exile. "The LORD will scatter you among all peoples, from one end of the earth to the other" (Deut 28:64). True, many Jews in the first century lived within the boundaries of the Promised Land, but even these did not possess the promises. Rather than exercising dominion over the land as a consequence of obedience, the Roman occupation was a daily reminder that the Promised Land did not belong to sinful Israel. This ongoing spiritual exile of the nation was the curse that Christ took upon himself at the cross as Israel's representative ("why have you forsaken me?").[10]

In any case, NPP writers generally agree, against traditional interpretation, that the curse of the Law does not refer to a deficiency in the Law or Judaism itself, to an impossible demand for moral perfection. Instead they see covenantal nomism at work, and blessing or curse is tied to faithfulness to the divine way revealed in the covenant.

DID PAUL HAVE A BURDENED OR A CLEAR CONSCIENCE?

From Martin Luther's "What must I do to find a gracious God?" to hymns like "He Touched Me," with the lines,

> Shackled by a heavy burden
> 'Neath a load of guilt and shame

10. Wright, *The Climax of the Covenant*, 146–47.

deliverance from a conscience burdened by sin and guilt has been central to many gospel presentations. Krister Stendahl, himself a Swedish Lutheran and important forerunner of the NPP, questioned whether this plight was an accurate depiction of the pre-Christian Saul/Paul.[11] Was it Judaism's inability to deliver him from the crushing burden of law-keeping which drove the Pharisee to the grace and free forgiveness in Christ?

A key text for Stendahl and the NPP is found in Phil 3:6, "as to righteousness under the law, blameless." This certainly doesn't sound too burdened. Alongside this statement of a rather robust conscience came others like,

> Brothers, up to this day I have lived my life with a clear conscience before God. (Acts 23:1; see also 24:16)

Sanders's covenantal nomism apparently worked just fine for the pre-Christian Saul. And of his post-conversion life he can testify,

> I am not aware of anything against myself. (1 Cor 4:4)

> Indeed, this is our boast, the testimony of our conscience: we have behaved in the world with frankness and godly sincerity. (2 Cor 1:12)

This idea of a robust versus burdened conscience prior to faith in Christ has not gone unchallenged. But before looking at three exegetical challenges, we should try and avoid a detour. Some might hear the NPP's view as a denial

11. Republished in 1976 (Stendahl, "Introspective Conscience"), the essay first appeared in English in 1963.

of their own experience and theology. Perhaps you were, indeed, "shackled by a heavy burden," and were set free by Christ's touch through faith. The aim of the NPP is not to deny that human beings can be tormented by a guilty conscience and can find in Christ forgiveness from this burden. The issue is not whether this describes *our* experience, but whether it accurately describes that of the first-century Pharisee Paul.

"Blameless" in Phil 3:6

So, on to the first challenge. Some try to understand Paul's claim to be blameless in Phil 3:6 differently. Perhaps blamelessness does not mean he thought he was OK before God (perfect?) in regard to law-keeping. Maybe it just means "blameless in the eyes of other human beings." Thus, Paul could say he was blameless before others, but still guilty and burdened before God. But since this seems lexically dubious to most interpreters,[12] the more common approach is to view this blamelessness as referring to how Paul *used to* view himself. Before Christ opened his eyes, he was unaware of his true sinfulness and actually thought he was righteous. Only now does he perceive that all his former reasons for "confidence in the flesh"—circumcision, Jewish heritage, Pharisaic righteousness—are, in fact, rubbish (Phil 3:4–8). Paul would never say as a Christian, "according to the Law, blameless." NPP authors reply, "Sure he would." See the verses about Paul's clear conscience above, or his expectation that he and others would live blamelessly in

12. As W. Grundmann notes of "blameless" for the Greek OT generally, "What is at issue is [blamelessness] before God" ("*Memphomai*," 572). See also, Kedar-Kopfstein, "*Tamam*," 707.

this world as Christians (Phil 2:15; 1 Thess 2:10; 1 Tim 3:10; etc.). Paul is not rejecting these badges of his Jewish identity, as though he now views them as bad or wrongheaded. He still holds that "circumcision is of value if you obey the law" (Rom 2:25) and that circumcision and Jewish heritage still hold great advantage (Rom 3:1–2). Rather, now that the fulfillment has come (Christ), it would constitute disobedience to the heavenly revelation to prefer that which was preparatory (Law, Judaism). Paul did, and still does, consider himself to have been blameless according to the righteousness in the Law, but in the light of Christ's coming (and only in that light), such blameless Jewish identity no longer marks out who belongs to the one God; it is in that context "rubbish." Both sides continue to debate the interpretation of this complex passage, so I will make no pretense to resolving it here.[13]

PAUL KNEW HE WAS A SINNER

As a second objection to this Paul, the blameless Pharisee, some would remind us that the apostle certainly did consider himself a "sinner," in fact, the "chief" (KJV) or "worst" (NIV) of them.

> The saying is sure and worthy of full acceptance, that Christ Jesus came into the world to save sinners—of whom I am the foremost. (1 Tim 1:15)

---

13. Those interested in pursuing the details of this particular exegetical debate might consult on the more traditional side, O'Brien, *The Epistle to the Philippians*; and on the NPP side, Dunn, "Philippians 3.2–14," 469–90.

Yes, indeed, Sinner with a capital S. But notice, Paul is not speaking here of a general sense of sinfulness, of difficulty in keeping the Law sufficiently. Here as elsewhere his Sin was quite specific and painful; it was his persecution of Yahweh's own people. He was "a blasphemer, a persecutor, and a man of violence" who "had acted ignorantly in unbelief" (1 Tim 1:13; see also Gal 1:13). Forever after it would remain for the apostle the greatest testimony to divine mercy that God had called one of his chief enemies to be one of his chief emissaries.

THE CONFLICTED PAUL IN ROMANS 7

A third objection to this blameless Paul stems from the conflict expressed in Romans 7.

> I do not understand my own actions. For I do not do what I want, but I do the very thing I hate. . . . For I know that nothing good dwells within me, that is, in my flesh. I can will what is right, but I cannot do it. For I do not do the good I want, but the evil I do not want is what I do. (Rom 7:15, 18–19)

On a traditional reading this speaks of the inner moral turmoil Paul experienced as a Jew trying to keep God's Law. Or, if Paul thought then that he was doing just fine, the passage expresses what he now knows about the futility and powerlessness of his former strivings since coming to Christ. Not only that, apart from the Spirit's empowerment it would still describe Paul's current experience. In the flesh he is still powerless and conflicted—"I know that nothing good dwells within me, that is, in my flesh. I can will what is right, but I cannot do it" (Rom 7:18). However, he has been rescued from this doomed situation—"Who will rescue me from this body of death? Thanks be to God through Jesus Christ our Lord!" (Rom 7:24–25). This piece of Pauline autobiography shows any sense of blamelessness to have been, and to still be, a delusion.

Students may be surprised to learn that this seemingly self-evident autobiographical interpretation has encountered some rough sledding.[14] Not only does a pre-conversion conflict seem to be in tension with Phil 3:6 ("blameless"), a converted Paul in such fleshly conflict does not fit easily with the sense of freedom in the Spirit he speaks of elsewhere.

> For the law of the Spirit of life in Christ Jesus has set you[15] free from the law of sin and of death. (Rom 8:2)

> But if you are led by the Spirit, you are not subject to the law. . . . The fruit of the Spirit is love, joy, peace, patience, kindness, generosity, faithfulness, gentleness, and self-control. There is no law against such things. And those who belong to Christ Jesus have crucified the flesh with its passions and desires. (Gal 5:18, 22–24)

In particular, Paul would hardly have characterized his pre-Christian Jewish existence as "once alive apart from the law" (Rom 7:9). For a large number of scholars, these

---

14. The original impetus for this interpretation is available only in German: Kümmel, *Römer 7*, 1–160. For a readable introduction to the issues, see Lambrecht, *The Wretched "I,"* 29–91.

15. Numerous Greek manuscripts read "me" instead of "you."

and other difficulties make the purely autobiographical interpretation untenable.

Instead of Paul's personal autobiography, the "I" could be rhetorical. It refers to some other person or group. Of course, to the extent that Paul identifies with this person or group, it also speaks of Paul, although not in an individual autobiographical sense. Paul has already done this in Romans when he writes, "if through *my* falsehood God's truthfulness abounds to his glory, why am *I* still being condemned as a sinner?" (Rom 3:7). The "*my*" is rhetorical, since it refers fundamentally to *Israel's* faithlessness (vv. 1–6), though Paul, of course, includes himself as part of Israel. Here in Romans 7 the rhetorical "I" could be

- humanity
- Adam (or adamic humanity)
- Israel

So, if the "I" is Israel, vv. 9–10 ("I was once alive apart from the law, but when the commandment came . . . I died") could refer to Israel's experience at Mt. Sinai. Israel had lived in the wilderness prior to the giving of Torah, but when Moses descended the mountain with the stone tablets, he discovered the nation's idolatry with the golden calf. The result was God's unwillingness to dwell with his people (only Moses got to actually "see" the Lord), all of whom (with two exceptions) died without entering the Promised Land. Or, if the "I" is Adam, v. 11 makes good sense—"Sin, seizing an opportunity in the commandment, deceived me and through it killed me." That is, echoing the language of Genesis 3, the serpent exploited the divine prohibition not to eat, deceived Adam (and Eve), and brought death to them.

It would take us too far afield to explore fully each of these possibilities. The point is simply that Romans 7 need not point to Paul's sense of pre-Christian sinfulness. Paul's robust conscience is preserved for the NPP.[16]

WORKS-BASED JUDAISM IN ROMANS 10:3

If Paul's Jewish background was so gracious, and not characterized by an attempt to earn divine approval by doing, why does he twice use language that seems to indicate the opposite? Speaking of the Jewish people in Romans, he states,

> For, being ignorant of the righteousness that comes from God, and seeking to establish their own, they have not submitted to God's righteousness. (Rom 10:3)

"Seeking to establish their own [righteousness]" certainly sounds like they were trying to earn their righteous status by obedience to the Law. And when speaking of himself in contrast to his former Jewish stance, Paul wants to

> be found in [Christ], not having a righteousness of my own that comes from the law, but one that comes through faith in Christ, the righteousness from God based on faith. (Phil 3:9)

Both passages appear to contrast the righteousness of God in Christ, which is given freely by grace, with one's "own righteousness," that which stems from oneself, from

16. For clarity, the rhetorical approach is not the NPP standard; just as traditional interpreters do not all favor the autobiographical. For example, D. Moo finds fault with many aspects of the NPP, yet himself favors a rhetorical approach to Romans 7 ("I" = Israel): Moo, "Israel and Paul in Romans 7:7–12," 122–35.

one's own doing and effort. It "comes from the law" rather than through "faith in Christ." Law versus Christ; working for one's own righteousness versus receiving it from God through faith in Christ; these are the contrasting options according to critics of the NPP.

Authors aligned with the NPP respond that the solution is actually fairly simple. When Paul says the righteousness of the Jewish people was "their own," this does not imply it was self-achieved by what they did. Rather, it was the righteousness that belonged to them as a people, it was characteristic of their covenant status. It was "their own," *their* Jewish covenantal righteous status, theirs as opposed to someone else's or some other sort.[17] That they sought to maintain or establish it, does not imply legalistic efforts, but the very reliance upon Jewish identity which Paul elsewhere criticizes as "boasting" or as "works of law" (Rom 3:27–31).[18] Their problem is not legalism, but ignorance in their commendable zeal for God (Rom 10:2). Wright's translation brings out the NPP sense nicely.

> They were ignorant, you see, of God's covenant faithfulness, and they were trying to establish a

17. This is the normal meaning of the Greek adjective used here (*idios*). Paul's reference to "my own" righteousness (Phil 3:9) might seem to point to individual achievement rather than group identity. However, since the entire paragraph has emphasized his solidarity with Jewish identity (Phil 3:2–11), he could simply mean "the righteousness which belongs to me as a zealous Jew."

18. "The verb ('establish') . . . denotes not . . . a bringing about of something which previously did not exist, but a . . . confirming of something which is already in existence. . . . they sought to establish and confirm what god had already given them" (Dunn, *Romans 9–16*, 595).

covenant status of their own; so they didn't submit to God's faithfulness.[19]

WORKS-RIGHTEOUSNESS FOR ABRAHAM IN ROMANS 4

For many opponents of the NPP, one text in particular proves fatal.[20]

> What then are we to say was gained by Abraham, our ancestor according to the flesh? For if Abraham was justified by works, he has something to boast about, but not before God. For what does the scripture say? "Abraham believed God, and it was reckoned to him as righteousness." Now to one who works, wages are not reckoned as a gift but as something due. But to one who without works trusts him who justifies the ungodly, such faith is reckoned as righteousness. (Rom 4:1–5)

Nothing is said of "works of law" in the sense of identity markers, only of "works" in the sense of human labor ("one who works") which are owed a "wage." The commercial tone of earning a wage by working seems palpable. Paul, then, contrasts such work with Abraham's faith which brought justification "as a gift" and "without works." What the NPP seeks to deny—the presence of a legalistic earning mentality based upon how much one has worked—seems to be plopped unmistakably in the middle of Paul's own argument.

19. Wright, *Paul for Everyone: Romans: Part 2*, 22. See further, Wright, "The Letter to the Romans," 654–55.

20. See, for example, Visscher, *Romans 4 and the New Perspective on Paul*.

Here is that contrast of faith (or gift) versus works which the Reformation highlighted and which Sanders and the NPP called into question for interpreting Paul and Judaism.

As with the exegesis of others Pauline texts, there is no standard NPP interpretation of Romans 4. However, such authors will usually point out that there is, indeed, a strong covenantal context to this section.[21] In 3:29–31 Paul noted that God justifies both Jews and Gentiles "by faith" rather than by "works of law." Since the identity of God's covenant people seemed to be tied up in the OT with Jewish identity ("works of law"), but Paul denies that connection, this raises the question which leads into chapter 4: "Do we then overthrow the law by this faith?" (Rom 3:31) The stage is set for him to look at the progenitor of the covenant people, Abraham, and to inquire whether he was justified by faith or by works (of law).

> What then are we to say was gained by Abraham, our ancestor according to the flesh? For if Abraham was justified by works, he has something to boast about, but not before God. (Rom 4:1–2)

The boasting in works here picks up the boasting in works of law spoken of only a bit earlier in 3:27–28, but now abbreviating "works of law" with the simple "works." That is, Jewish identity markers ("works of law") are in view, not meritorious human efforts. Paul, then, quotes Gen 15:6 ("Abraham believed God, and it was reckoned to him as righteousness") to make the point, "It was not faithful Abraham to whom God gave the promise, but Abraham the

21. See especially the treatment of Romans 4 in Wright, "The Letter to the Romans."

type of the ungodly-idolater-become-proselyte."[22] Abraham was granted the promises, was justified, while still uncircumcised, technically an "ungodly" Gentile. Only later (Gen 17) does Jewish identity via circumcision come into play (see Rom 4:9–12).

This still leaves the problematic verse 4 unexplained. "Now to one who works, wages are not reckoned as a gift but as something due." How do NPP authors avoid the idea of "earning salvation" that seems to lie in this text? Typically they will argue that this commercial metaphor (wages are earned not given as a gift) is a subordinate point in Paul's argument and should not be elevated to the position of some central theological datum.[23] Dunn adds, this reckoning as a gift versus as a calculation of prior faithfulness refers to Abraham's *initial* justification, whereas traditional interpretation usually has *final* justification in view ("saved by works"). The point is actually quite simple: God's initial reckoning of Abraham to be righteous occurred prior to (apart from, without) any acts of faithfulness, any works, on his part.

EPHESIANS 2:8–10; 2 TIMOTHY 1:9; TITUS 3:5–6

Several passages from the disputed letters of Paul seem to point unmistakably to precisely the grace-versus-works contrast that the NPP says was not in Paul's mind.

22. Dunn, "The New Perspective on Paul: Whence, What, and Whither?" 48.

23. "Paul's main argument is that 'works' (i.e., of Torah) were not the reason for Abraham's justification; and the idea of 'working' is then expanded metaphorically in vv. 4–5 into the idea of doing a job for which one earns wages." Wright, "The Letter to the Romans," 490.

> For by grace you have been saved through faith, and this is not your own doing; it is the gift of God—not the result of works, so that no one may boast. (Eph 2:8–9)

> [God] saved us and called us with a holy calling, not according to our works but according to his own purpose and grace. (2 Tim 1:9)

> He saved us, not because of any works of righteousness that we had done, but according to his mercy. (Tit 3:5)

Surely these texts presume that someone was asserting salvation through "your own doing," because of one's own works of righteousness rather than the gift and mercy of God. "The writer wishes to exclude any notion of earning salvation by human efforts which lead to self-congratulation."[24]

In spite of the clear challenge to the NPP posed by these verses, writers aligned with this perspective have been "strangely silent," in some cases because these passages are not considered Pauline.[25] Of the few responses by NPP writers, the following represents a common approach.

> The "works" by which the people of God are not saved in [Eph 2:9] is shorthand for "the works of the law." As such these works are not the "good works" to which God's people have been called in verse ten. That the Jew/Gentile issue is still in view is clear from what follows in 2:11—3:13.[26]

24. Lincoln, "Ephesians 2:8–10," 628.

25. Weedman, "Reading Ephesians," 81.

26. Mattison, "Confronting Legalism or Exclusivism?" Similarly Thompson, *The New Perspective on Paul*, 17.

Thus, even though the phrase "works of law" is not used in these passages, they are addressing the same type of controversy as found in Galatians and Romans.[27]

WHAT ABOUT *PISTIS CHRISTOU*?

Another debate often brought into proximity with NPP discussions concerns the meaning of a Greek phrase used by Paul: *pistis christou* ("faith of Christ," KJV). Translation options include

- "faith in Christ"—the "objective genitive" solution, since "Christ" is the object of faith, or
- "faithfulness of Christ"—the "subjective genitive" solution, since "Christ" is the subject of faith (or faithfulness).

The difference should be clear when applied to a specific Pauline text.

> We know that a person is justified not by the works of the law but through faith in Jesus Christ. (Gal 2:16)

The cited NRSV translation, along with most modern English versions, opts for the objective genitive.[28] Our "faith in

27. Another possibility—these verses focus on the initial entry into the saved or elect people ("called us with a holy calling") rather than on the final obtaining of salvation. The question being answered in these passages is not "What do I have to do in order to make it into heaven?" but "What caused God to love, call, elect and save me in the first place?" The answer is, "nothing but God's undeserved mercy."

28. An interesting exception is the KJV, which translates "by the faith of Jesus Christ." This has been "corrected" in the NKJV to "by faith in Jesus Christ."

Jesus Christ" contrasts with (our) works of law. This could obviously (though not necessarily, see below) merge seamlessly into the traditional contrast between faith and works.

The NET Bible, on the other hand, along with a large number of modern commentators, chooses the subjective genitive and translates, "we know that no one is justified by the works of the law but by the faithfulness of Jesus Christ." The "faith of Christ" translation seems to weaken the faith-versus-works contrast, and, thus, could be viewed as the NPP option. This is, however, not the case. There is, in fact, no standard NPP position on this debate. Dunn takes the "faith in Christ" position and says the choice is only tangential to the NPP.[29] Wright takes the "faithfulness of Christ" position; Christ carries out the covenant faithfulness at which Israel failed. Both sides acknowledge the presence in Paul of the other; those arguing for the "faith of Christ" are clear that our faith in Christ is not thereby made irrelevant; and those arguing for "faith in Christ" are clear that the ground of justification is Christ's life and death, not our faith. A particular decision on this issue is not necessary for the NPP.[30]

29. Dunn, "In Search of Common Ground," 292n16.

30. For further details, see the essays by Richard Hays and James Dunn in Hays, *The Faith of Jesus Christ*, 249–97.

7

THEOLOGICAL CONCERNS

IF THE debates covered in the previous two chapters tend-
ed to be of more interest to academics, the theological
issues raised about the NPP in this chapter have definitely
gotten the interest of a broader audience. These are the matters discussed with considerable fervor on church Web sites,
in sermons, and in books and pamphlets on Paul aimed at a
more general church audience.

> At stake is nothing less than the gospel itself, the
> church's proclamation of the good news of salva-
> tion in Christ. [. . .] The new perspective ulti-
> mately offers a different gospel than that to which
> the Reformation bore witness.[1]

> The current revision of the doctrine of justi-
> fication as formulated by the advocates of the

1. Venema, *The Gospel of Free Acceptance in Christ*, ix–x.

so-called New Perspective on Paul is nothing less than a fundamental repudiation not just of that Protestantism which seeks to stand within the creedal and doctrinal trajectories of the Reformation but also of virtually the entire Western tradition on justification from at least as far back as Augustine.[2]

Rejection of the Reformation . . . is a big plank of the New Perspective.[3]

REJECTION OF THE PROTESTANT REFORMATION?

The Reformation tradition's approach to Paul is fundamentally wrong.[4]

If this quotation is typical of NPP writers, it is not hard to see why Christians aligned with the Protestant Reformation, especially its Lutheran and Reformed branches, feel attacked by the NPP. Thus, one writer subtitled his book on the NPP, "The 'Lutheran Paul' and His Critics."[5]

On one level, a response to this charge is simple. Some NPP writers do, in fact, see their stance as challenging, or even overturning, the central insights of the Protestant Reformation. Others most definitely do not.[6] On the personal

2. Trueman, "The Portrait of Martin Luther in Contemporary New Testament Scholarship," 1.

3. Zahl, "Mistakes of the New Perspective on Paul," 7.

4. Watson, *Paul, Judaism, and the Gentiles*, 1.

5. Westerholm, *Perspectives Old and New on Paul*.

6. For a Reformation-friendly defense of the NPP, see Garlington, *In Defense of the New Perspective on Paul*, 9–11.

level, this charge turns out to be sometimes on target, and other times inaccurate slander. The reason, as should be clear from chapter 4, is that the persons holding the NPP represent a fair variety of opinions on quite a number of issues.

Since "we reject the Reformation" is hardly a typical statement of NPP proponents, those who make this charge usually have something much more specific in mind.

DOES THE NPP DENY LUTHER'S CENTRAL INSIGHT ABOUT JUSTIFICATION BY GRACE ALONE THROUGH FAITH ALONE?

Since the doctrine of justification by faith alone is probably the *sine qua non* of the Reformation, it is understandable that anything that impinges on this conviction may be viewed as a serious threat. Thus, one well-known pastor-scholar recently wrote an entire book detailing how N. T. Wright's position amounts to a repudiation of the Reformation's understanding of justification.[7] Wright has published a book-length reply defending his Reformational orthodoxy, and other NPP authors have been equally insistent that their position on justification is not anti-Lutheran.[8] So, what are the real issues here, and how do NPP authors respond?

JUSTIFICATION NO LONGER AT THE CENTER

First, is justification by faith the organizing centerpiece of Paul's theology? This has generally been the way the Reformation tradition has understood Paul. It has not been

---

7. Piper, *The Future of Justification*.
8. Wright, *Justification*; Dunn and Suggate, *The Justice of God*.

the way NPP authors have read him. Although most of the latter do not wish to downgrade justification to a "subsidiary crater" in Paul's thought,[9] they do move it from this center position. However, in fairness to the NPP, whether this actually amounts to a repudiation of the Reformation is an open matter among experts in Reformation history and theology. Divine sovereignty and union with Christ may have functioned, arguably, as more of an organizing center for John Calvin than justification, and Luther's "center" is equally under consideration.[10]

DENIAL OF FORENSIC JUSTIFICATION

Second, does the NPP deny forensic justification? For those unfamiliar with this terminology, part of the Reformation's genius was the discovery that God declares the sinner to be righteous based upon the work of Christ accepted in simple faith. Thus, justification refers to the declaration by God that a believing sinner is now considered righteous, acquitted. "Forensic" refers to a legal or law-court setting; thus, forensic justification is like a judge pronouncing the "not guilty" verdict. Unrighteous sinners can be pronounced "not guilty" or righteous because of Christ's death and resurrection. Sinners "do" nothing to attain this verdict, they simply accept it by faith in the gospel proclamation. Luther's Catholic opponents ridiculed this as a legal fiction and insisted that God does not merely *declare* a sinner to

9. This was Albert Schweitzer's term for what, to him, was a secondary concept used by Paul only when battling against certain Jewish opponents.

10. See Kennedy, *Union with Christ*; and Braaten and Jenson, *Union with Christ*.

be righteous, but actually *makes* that sinner righteous. That is, in Roman Catholic theology, justification is not merely forensic, it is also transformative. For Luther, however, to make justification in any way dependent upon even the least bit of ethical transformation, even the least amount of good works in the sinner's transformed life, dashes all confidence in justification by faith alone. How transformed do I need to be, he asks back, in order to have some assurance that I have, indeed, been justified?

Since we will take a look at the relation of justification to sanctification (ethical transformation) below, let's return to the question of the NPP and forensic justification. Both Dunn and Wright acknowledge the forensic character of justification. They question, however, whether this is a sufficient description in and of itself.[11]

No More Imputation of Righteousness

This brings us immediately to the third justification-related issue: does the NPP deny imputed righteousness? Here again, a brief explanation is needed. If sinners are not in themselves righteous, and if God will not pronounce the wicked to be righteous ("for I will not acquit the guilty" Exod 23:7), how will he justify the ungodly? The answer: God will take the perfect righteousness of Jesus Christ and will credit ("reckon") it to the account of the sinner. When God looks at the believer, he sees not a sinner but a person clothed in Christ's righteousness. An exchange has occurred: Christ takes the believer's sins, and the believer is credited with

11. See, for instance, Wright, *What Saint Paul Really Said*, esp. ch. 7.

Christ's righteousness. Rather than pronouncing a sinner to be righteous, God sees a righteous one whom he rightfully acquits. The key text here is Gen 15:6, which Paul cites in Rom 4:3, "Abraham believed God, and it was reckoned to him [imputed] as righteousness."

So, does the NPP deny this doctrine of imputation? The answer is, some do and some don't.[12] For most, it appears to be somewhat beside the point for interpreting key Pauline texts. Thus, commenting on "it was reckoned to him as righteousness" in Rom 4:3, N. T. Wright comments, "God counted Abraham's faith as constituting covenant membership."[13] Since righteousness here for Wright does not refer to Christ's perfect obedience to the Law, but to covenant membership, the issue of crediting Christ's righteousness to Abraham's account is simply not in view.

The larger problem with this charge is that the same answer ("some do, some don't") applies to theologians and biblical scholars apart from the NPP debate. Thus, Robert Gundry, a New Testament scholar who would by no means reckon himself to the NPP, has challenged the idea that Paul taught imputation.[14] And imputation has not been universally held among theological heirs of the Protestant Reformation.[15] More fundamentally, this particular aspect

12. Don Garlington, for example, prefers "union with Christ" to imputation. See Garlington, "Imputation or Union with Christ?"

13. Wright, "The Letter to the Romans," 491.

14. Gundry, "The Nonimputation of Christ's Righteousness," 17–45. The entire volume is an excellent introduction to the larger debate going on regarding imputation. A response is found in the same volume: Carson, "The Vindication of Imputation," 46–78.

15. See Warfield, "Imputation," 465–67. Neither the Anglican nor Wesleyan traditions, for example, line up with Luther on this issue.

of the debate hinges upon identifying "the Reformation doctrine of imputation," as though there were consensus among the early reformers on this matter.[16] To charge the NPP with being "against the Reformation" because some proponents reject a particular understanding of imputation is rather unfair. The charge should really be, "Some NPP proponents reject what some Reformational theologians hold as essential to the Reformation."

ARE WE SNEAKING SALVATION BY GOOD WORKS (LEGALISM) BACK IN BY THE SIDE ENTRANCE?

This is unquestionably the fundamental concern about the NPP from a pastoral and theological side, since it affects so many other areas. If our final salvation is in some way connected to—that is, dependent upon—our behavior, our good works, will not all the comfort and assurance won by Luther and the Reformation be lost? If it is not faith *alone* that secures our justification, both in the beginning and in the ultimate judgment, but faith *plus* any amount of obedience, then we can never have any confident assurance of our salvation in this life. If we think that to our faith we must add some amount of obedience in order to be ultimately saved, we will fall inescapably into the very legalism from which the Reformation rescued us.

Most of these critics of the NPP will be quick to add, this is not to make Christian obedience unimportant, as though one could exercise saving faith in Christ, and thereafter live like the devil. Far from it. There will be no final

16. Fink, "Was There a 'Reformation Doctrine of Justification'?" 205–35.

justification without a corresponding sanctification. The Reformers were always careful not to separate justification and sanctification. Neither can exist without the other. But neither dare they be confused or mixed. Justification is by faith alone; although sanctification must inevitably follow from it in the Christian's life, this subsequent life of obedience impinges in no way upon the believer's justification by faith. These two realms must be kept distinct (not separate!), else all is lost.[17]

As with the challenges regarding justification, this one, too, is a bit more complex than it sounds at first. It is also worth reminding readers that the NPP is primarily a matter of NT interpretation, of biblical studies. The concerns of its proponents are first of all, and sometimes solely, issues of "What did Paul say and mean?" rather than pastoral questions ("How will this affect ministry and Christian experience today?"). Thus, remembering again the diversity among NPP writers, this charge may be of

17. Don Garlington suggested to me in private correspondence that differentiating the *ordo salutis* and *historia salutis* might be helpful here. The *ordo salutis* refers to the logical ordering of distinct theological elements in salvation. For instance, do we exercise saving faith prior to being regenerated, or does human depravity mean that some divine "making alive" must happen first (at least logically)? The *historia salutis* refers to our experience of this salvation process, in which case many of these elements appear to occur simultaneously and somewhat indistinguishably. Even if regeneration does precede faith logically (something not all Christian traditions would accept), in our own experience we certainly do not recommend waiting to perceive some inner transformation before believing in Christ. Thus, those stressing the strict distinguishing of justification and sanctification might be concerned particularly with the *ordo salutis*, while those warning against their separation may be thinking especially of the *historia salutis*.

importance to some proponents, and beside the point to others. What follows seeks to represent the typical responses of the former group.

ASSURANCE AND THE NPP

First, does the NPP damage Christian assurance of salvation?[18] The answer is "no," but it does preserve the difference between true and false assurance, or in the language of Reformation-era debates, between the assurance of faith (Latin *certitudo*) and an iron-clad subjective (or intellectual) certainty (Latin *securitas*). Martin Luther himself noted that the latter *securitas* "cancels out faith."[19] That is, a subjective certainty, a presumptuous self-confidence, ruins faith. Thinking we know something for certain is not the same as faith. In fact, knowing something generally makes faith that it is true unnecessary. The reverse is equally true: "the assurance of faith, *certitudo fidei* . . . excludes false confidence, *securitas*."[20] This joyful confidence cannot be divorced from trust, from faith; that's why it is called "assurance *of faith*." For this confidence we do not look within ourselves to see if we have such "knowledge" or "certainty" (*securitas*). Rather, we look away from ourselves to Christ; we reach out, grab hold, and hang on. This is the assurance of a small child hanging from a tree limb twelve feet off the

18. "Christian assurance is pushed to the periphery of Christian experience. According to the New Perspective, salvation is intrinsically uncertain (if not elusive) whilst it relies upon the instrument of our unpredictable obedience." Middleton, "Pastoral Implications."

19. M. Luther, *Die fünfte Disputation gegen die Antinomer*, 1538, WA 39/1, 356, 25; cited in Jüngel, *Justification*, 246.

20. Jüngel, *Justification*, 246.

ground, whose father says, "Let go, I'll catch you." The child is thrilled her father is there and she is confident in him, but nervous as a cat all the same. (This is how assurance and the fear of the Lord coexist.)

PAUL SOFT ON LEGALISM

Second, and returning to the larger concern that the NPP may sneak good works back into salvation, by interpreting "works of law" as marks of Jewish identity rather than good works Paul no longer seems to be opposing salvation by good deeds (legalism). The NPP makes Paul soft on legalism. Not so fast, protest NPP proponents. True, Paul is not opposing good deeds in the verses normally cited on this point. But that certainly does mean he now favors salvation by works. As a Jewish theologian he would have found it ludicrous to imagine that frail human creatures could earn the divine favor by their efforts, that they could somehow put God in their debt. Even if Paul does not polemicize against legalism in the verses normally cited, this does not mean he wouldn't have done so given the opportunity. Legalism simply wasn't the issue confronting him in his churches, and thus we find little opposition to it in his letters.

THE NPP BLURS THE DISTINCTION BETWEEN ROMAN CATHOLIC AND PROTESTANT SOTERIOLOGY

This criticism overlaps considerably with the concerns about justification by faith noted earlier. There are, however, a couple of additional matters of importance here. One has to do with ecumenism and the other with synergism.

A FORM OF ECUMENISM

Discussions between Lutherans and Roman Catholics over justification point to a blurring of sharp Reformational distinctives and a readiness to speak of convergence.[21] The NPP moves in the same direction. Covenantal nomism and NPP versions of salvation seem closer to Roman Catholic views than to Luther's. They certainly highlight the role of obedience more than "by grace alone through faith alone" would seem to do. Does this portend eventual reunification of these divided portions of Christendom? Such ecumenical union sounds to many like the clearest signal that the gains of the Reformation are being lost.

Apart from the personal views of varied NPP scholars (some probably lean toward ecclesiastical reunification, others do not), the issue of concern here is whether the positions taken by the NPP tend toward such ecumenical reunion or not. The online "Paul Page" (www.thepaulpage.com) states as one of the NPP "promises": "Build common ground between Catholics and Protestants." Since the NPP focuses on biblical studies, rather than on theology or ecumenical relations, this refers not to ecclesiastical union, but to issues in the Pauline letters such as the meaning of "works of law," "righteousness," "faith of (or in) Christ," "grace," etc. These undoubtedly have theological and ecumenical implications, but those implications are not usually the driving force behind such studies or findings. NPP writings are trying to get "back to Paul," not "back to Rome" or "Luther" or any other theological movement or church historical period. NPP positions do, indeed, allow for greater rapprochement

21. Reumann and Fitzmyer, *Righteousness in the New Testament*.

between Protestant and Roman Catholic biblical studies, but that is probably because neither side is aiming primarily to find a "Protestant Paul" or a "Catholic Paul."

SLIDING BACK TO SYNERGISM

Critics suspect, second, that the NPP represents a form of synergism not unlike that alleged of the Roman Catholic Church.[22] This theological term comes from two Greek words meaning "to work" (*erg-*) "together" (*syn*). The doctrine of synergism holds that human salvation results from the working together of God and the human person. Its opposite, monergism, holds that God alone is the effective agent in human salvation. In monergism, the human is passive. He or she must indeed do something, must receive in faith what God has done, but that reception is not really a human work. Even that reception, that exercise of saving faith, is a gift from God.[23]

On the face of it, critics seem to have a simple case. Although Sanders's covenantal nomism stressed that Jews "get in" by divine grace alone (election), they "stay in" by obedience to Torah. This certainly seems to indicate that final salvation occurs only as a result of the two agents working together, i.e., by synergism.

Authors aligned with the NPP respond in a number of ways. First, although divine–human working together in salvation (synergism) is a negative term in much church

22. On this particular debate, see Yinger, "Reformation Redivivus: Synergism and the New Perspective," 89–106.

23. Monergism.com provides many resources defending this perspective.

historical and theological discussion, Paul seems to find room for it.

> . . . work out your own salvation with fear and trembling. (Phil 2:12)

And in numerous places he seems to indicate that human working together with grace is a necessary condition for the ultimate reception of salvation.[24] Second, while Luther did reject the alleged semi-Pelagianism of contemporary Roman Catholicism and generally seemed to favor monergism, the monergism-versus-synergism scheme of NPP critics masks far more complex Reformation debates over the same. Significant portions of the Reformation tradition expressed their discomfort with the language of monergism (Melanchthon and Wesley, for instance), and saw some type of evangelical synergism as a better descriptor.[25]

INDIVIDUAL SALVATION NO LONGER MATTERS

This concern stems particularly from the emphasis among NPP writers on sociological or group identity categories. Is the gospel mainly about how one is identified with the right group—being identified with the covenant people by Christ-faith or by Jewish marks—or is it mainly about "grace abounding to sinners"? Is the gospel's chief end to save the unrighteous or to break down ethnic barriers? When Paul says justification is not by works of law, is he merely rejecting the sufficiency of Jewish identity markers,

24. See Rom 8:13, 17; 10:9; 11:22; 1 Cor 3:17; 15:2; Gal 5:2; also Col 1:22–23; 2 Tim 2:12.

25. See Rakestraw, "John Wesley as a Theologian of Grace," 193–203; and Olson, *The Mosaic of Christian Belief*, 277–86.

or is he rejecting the individual sinner's attempt to earn salvation by human effort?

Some NPP writers do seem to jettison much interest in individual salvation. Of course, their point is that this individualistic focus represents a non-Pauline and modern Western way of viewing the world. Ancients understood themselves (i.e., as individuals) in terms of family and national heritage—group identity—rather than first answering the call to "know thyself" and then defining their group identity.

Others, however, resist this reductionism (everything reduced to sociological matters) as a "false dichotomy" and call for more of a both/and position.

> . . . to belong to the new covenant is to be among the community of the saved. And justification does, in fact, tell us how to be saved, in that it depicts God's method of saving sinners—by faith in Christ, not by works of the law—and placing them in covenant standing with himself.[26]

A SHORT CONCLUDING ASIDE

Readers may have noticed that many of these theological critiques are quite complex and difficult to unravel vis-à-vis the NPP. The concerns of critics arise largely from the realms of church history and systematic theology, not directly from biblical studies. But NPP writers usually see themselves as biblical scholars, and less as theologians. Some of the tension we have felt in these more theological debates is the tension felt when moving from the biblical text (i.e., what it meant

26. Garlington, "The New Perspective on Paul," 11–12.

in that context) to the horizon of our theology and church praxis. The questions we raise in these latter spheres—Does Paul care about individual salvation? Does Paul reject legalism and synergism?—may or may not be the questions Paul himself is raising in his letters. Non-NPP authors tend to find more-or-less direct evidence in Paul's letters in answer to our theological questions. One argument runs, "Since human nature hasn't changed all that much in the past 2,000 years, surely Paul faced some of the same human questions we face." NPP writers tend to stress the differences in Paul's situation from ours (or from Luther's), including the major cultural (i.e., human) differences, and find Paul answering different questions from ours. Just as NPP authors are generally ready to try and interpret and apply Paul's answers to our questions, so non-NPP authors are aware of the cultural differences between Paul's and our situations. That is, the difference between the two approaches is hardly as black and white as it may sometimes appear. Nevertheless, the adjustment in emphasis can often have major ramifications.

In the case of imputation, for example, there are only a few biblical texts that seem directly relevant.[27] Of course, supporters of imputation in church history and theology argue that the doctrine is implied by these and other texts and by the logic of forensic justification. Non-NPP writers can agree that all this may, indeed, be true (or not). However, it goes beyond the immediate ken of biblical studies, which is mostly interested in "what Paul meant." Barring clearer statements from Paul's letters, biblical scholars will generally stop short of constructing a full doctrine and mechanism of atonement. For scholars of church history and theology

27. Gen 15:6; Ps 106:31; Rom 4:3–6, 9–11, 22–24.

this is not enough. Biblical studies may deliver the building blocks, but these blocks cannot be left lying around, they must be sorted and organized into a coherent structure. As you can see, the tasks of biblical studies and theology are obviously related, but are not quite the same. The one seeks to hew the building blocks out of the Pauline texts; the other seeks to organize these blocks into a structure that is coherent and helpful for questions being asked now. There is little evidence in Paul's letters that he was exercised by the question of imputation; this was a question that became central during the Reformation. Trying to get Paul to answer a question he wasn't asking always produces discomfort for biblical scholars, and usually unsatisfying results for theologians.

8

LET'S HEAR IT FOR THE NPP
POSITIVE EFFECTS

Now that we have given what I hope is a fair consideration of the various concerns raised by the NPP, it is time to ask about the positive value of this interpretive trend. If the NPP has got things largely right concerning first-century Judaism and Paul's relationship to it, so what? Does this really make much difference today? This final chapter collects various hints dropped in earlier chapters and says "yes."

BETTER GRASP ON PAUL'S LETTERS

The most obvious result comes whenever we pick up a NT and read one of Paul's letters. In verse after verse a NPP interpretation will allow us to get closer to what the apostle was actually trying to say. Was Paul nervous about legalism, about self-righteous good works, when he said "not by works of law but by faith in Jesus Christ" (Gal 2:16)? Or, with the NPP, was his concern primarily with whether Gentiles had to become Jewish? And when he then praises the doing of good works—"if you sow to the Spirit, you will reap eternal life from the Spirit. So let us not grow weary in doing what is right, for we will reap at harvest time" (Gal 6:8–9)—we do not have to switch gears, but can see Paul's love of good works running consistently through all he says. (See chapter 6 for further examples of the difference in interpretation made by the NPP.)

AVOIDING WESTERN INDIVIDUALISM

A New Perspective reading of Paul's letters can also help reduce the Western overemphasis on the individual. The gospel is no longer all about my salvation; instead, it is about a new creation (2 Cor 5:17) and a new people. Romans 7 need no longer be primarily about my personal struggle with Sin, but about Law and Sin in Israel's (or Adam's) history. Of course, this doesn't have to eliminate "me" from the picture altogether. It just moves me out of the center.

GOODBYE TO ANTI-SEMITISM?

The NPP might also help reduce some Christian tendencies toward anti-Semitism or anti-Judaism. Rather than speaking of inferior Jewish legalism, covenantal nomism sounds a more positive note toward Christianity's mother-religion. Rather than a failed or wrong-headed pattern of religion, Judaism and Christianity turn out to have most of their pattern in common. The main discontinuity, of course, remains Jesus Christ. For some NPP proponents this means the complete rejection of supersessionism: that is, the church does not replace Israel in God's plan for humanity; Israel and the church are now on equal footing before God (with or without Jesus Christ). For others, like myself, Israel is reconfigured (rather than replaced) to include both Jew and Gentile in the Israel reconstituted in Messiah Jesus; but it is still paramount that one be part of this Israel, children of Abraham. To non-Christian Jews this will probably still sound like the old supersessionism, since Israel as they understand her is no longer adequate. But the "no longer adequate" is built not upon some inherent flaw in Israel's religion, as with most earlier versions of supersessionism, but upon a Christian conviction that God has begun a new era in Israel's history with Jesus Christ.

MOVING FROM OLD TO NEW TESTAMENT MADE EASIER

In a similar vein, the NPP makes quite a difference in formulating a biblical theology. With it there is considerably more continuity between OT and NT. Paul's message is not the antithesis of Judaism (or of the OT Law) but is a christologically reconfigured continuation or climax of the same. This allows Christians to read their OT's more naturally. Think, for example, about how you might read Psalm 18. It begins easily enough with "I love you, O LORD, my strength. The LORD is my rock, my fortress, and my deliverer" (vv. 1–2). Christians can repeat this with hardly a second thought. But a bit further along it turns troublesome.

> The LORD rewarded me according to my righteousness; according to the cleanness of my hands he recompensed me. For I have kept the ways of

> the LORD, and have not wickedly departed from
> my God. For all his ordinances were before me,
> and his statutes I did not put away from me. I
> was blameless before him, and I kept myself from
> guilt. Therefore the LORD has recompensed me
> according to my righteousness, according to the
> cleanness of my hands in his sight. (Ps 18:20–24)

Traditionally, Christian interpreters have winced at the seeming self-righteousness of this passage, or have re-interpreted "my righteousness" as the imputed righteousness of Christ. The NPP might, however, allow Christians to recite this whole Psalm without such efforts. The righteousness and blamelessness in the psalm refer not to some sort of self-righteous perfection, but to the integrity of faithful conduct expected everywhere in the Bible, including the New Testament. It is the loyalty (= faith or faithfulness) inspired by God's grace, and speaks of those who are "loyal" and who "take refuge in him" (vv. 25, 30).[1] The psalmist is simply saying, "I have not turned my back on you, Lord, but have sought to walk in your ways. Please deal with me according to the gracious promises of your covenant."

PAUL AND JESUS ON THE SAME PAGE

Not only does the NPP ease the transition from Old to New Testament (though the coming of Jesus as messiah will always remain as a climactic intrusion), but it also puts Paul and Jesus on speaking terms. There has been much talk of Paul founding a new religion, Christianity, which replaced the simple Galilean Jewish message of Jesus. As some put the matter, Jesus sought the renewal, or reform, of Judaism;

---

1. See Kwakkel, *According to My Righteousness*.

Paul abandoned that aim and sought the creation of a world religion encompassing Gentiles. Jesus preached the imminent kingdom of God; Paul preached Jesus—the proclaimer became the proclaimed. For Jesus every "jot and tittle" was important (Matt 5:18), while Paul felt the Law had come to an end (Rom 10:4). Jesus called people to rigorous discipleship if they would enter God's kingdom; Paul called them to simple faith. You get the drift.

One does not necessarily have to adopt the NPP in order to reconcile Jesus and Paul, but the NPP offers some helpful tools. Instead of viewing Pauline grace in competition with gospel discipleship, covenantal nomism shows them forming a harmonious pattern in both Jesus and Paul (and Judaism). Both held to the foundational importance of grace. The laborers in the vineyard (Matt 20:1–16) do not receive their pay according the number of hours worked, but according to divine generosity. Jesus's healings were vivid demonstrations that God's favor was being showered upon the seemingly unworthy. Paul's commitment to grace needs no further comment.

But alongside this stress on grace came an emphasis on the necessity of obedience. In Jesus's judgment parable (Matt 25:31–46) the destiny of the sheep and goats—eternal punishment or eternal life—is based upon their obedience to Jesus's way: feeding the hungry, visiting prisoners, etc. And Paul is still convinced that God "will repay according to each one's deeds: to those who by patiently doing good seek for glory and honor and immortality, he will give eternal life" (Rom 2:6–7).

When "works" are thought of negatively—meritorious or self-righteous good works—reconciling this dual emphasis on grace and obedience proves more difficult. Covenantal nomism suggests that these two focal points cohered in Judaism as well as in Jesus and Paul. The gospel that Paul preached turns out to follow the same pattern as that of Jesus.

Another point of continuity between Paul and Jesus suggested by the NPP concerns the saving significance of membership in the nation of Israel. In much Reformational exegesis Romans 9–11 (What about Israel's Election?) seemed an odd fit with Paul's exploration of individual justification by grace through faith (chs. 1–8). The NPP suggests that questions about covenant membership are, in fact, the driving force behind Paul's gospel discussions (especially in Romans and Galatians). Does one have to be, or to become, Jewish, perform the "works of the law," in order to be in Christ? This is, then, reminiscent of Jesus's consistent message that Jewish identity is no safeguard from the coming wrath. His first sermon in Luke's Gospel almost led to his demise because he taught that God would give no preferential treatment to the descendants of Abraham (Luke 4:25–30). This echoes the preaching of John the Baptist, "Do not begin to say to yourselves, 'We have Abraham as our ancestor'; for I tell you, God is able from these stones to raise up children to Abraham" (Luke 3:8). Thus, Paul continues one of Jesus's central themes as central to his own gospel.

PATCHING UP OLD CHURCH WOUNDS

As a last benefit of the NPP to be mentioned, reconciliation between Catholics and Protestants over justification might just be possible. Since the Lutheran Reformation's understanding of Paul and justification was one of the major elements leading to the split with Rome,[2] the NPP's re-evaluation of Paul and justification might show the two sides not quite so far apart on this matter as Luther thought.

You should now be well-equipped to answer the questions raised at the beginning of this book.

- Where did the NPP come from?
- What is it (simple description)?
- What are some of its potential dangers?
- What are some of its potential benefits?

But more importantly these pages may have forced you back to Paul's writings themselves. These debates are largely an attempt to get back to this Old Perspective, that is, to Paul's own perspective on God, Christ, the Law, faith, etc. Supporters of the NPP usually consider their position not really "new," but a recovery of that older, truly Pauline understanding. Many of the opponents see a major rediscovery of Paul already in the Reformation, with the NPP being, therefore, a new departure. The answer, for both sides, lies in an ongoing engagement with the apostle Paul and his letters. That, by all admissions, has been a positive result of the New Perspective.

---

2. There were, and are of course, other elements to this division: sacraments, ordained ministry, celibacy, etc.

The Conversation Continues

AFTERWORD
BY DONALD A. HAGNER[1]

IT WOULD be hard to think of a more exciting and challenging, not to say revolutionary, development in Pauline studies of the modern era than the emergence of the New Perspective on Paul. Every student of Paul needs to know about the New Perspective, its roots, its pros and cons. Dr. Yinger has therefore done us a great service in producing this succinct and helpful guide. He is himself an expert in this field and his presentation is clear, fair, and authoritative.

As Yinger points out, the New Perspective on Paul finds its beginnings in the stress upon a new and more adequate understanding of Judaism, as not a legalistic religion, i.e., where one attempts to earn one's salvation by

1. Don Hagner and Don Garlington wrote their afterwords in response to *The New Perspective on Paul: An Introduction*, and without knowledge of what the other had written.

righteous deeds, but like Christianity, as a religion of grace, where salvation is granted by God as a gift.

Judaism ideally conceived—not necessarily as always practiced!—is a religion of grace, wherein God chooses to save a people apart from their merits. God freely chooses the Jews as his people; election is at the heart of Judaism. And he sticks with them despite their habitual disobedience.

This better understanding of Judaism, as outlined in this volume, was described by E. P. Sanders as a "covenantal nomism," that is, a Law-centeredness (hence, nomism) but within the larger framework of the covenant(s), i.e., an act (or acts) of God's grace. A nomist is one whose life is centered on obedience to the Law, but not to earn acceptance with God. The covenantal nomist starts with acceptance by God. This is surely an accurate characterization of the theology and soteriology of the OT and much of the Second Temple literature, i.e., of the time of Jesus and the Apostles. But a problem emerges in the post-exilic period. Given the repentant mood of the nation and their intense rededication to obeying the Law of Moses, the balance between Law and covenant was often lost. The Law became practically an obsession, as we can see in groups such as the Pharisees and the Essenes, and the effect of this zeal for the Law could sometimes be that the bedrock of grace was neglected or simply forgotten.

A key question in evaluating the New Perspective is whether or not there were Jewish legalists in the Second Temple period who (in contrast to the nomists mentioned in the preceding paragraph) did not understand their religion well enough to realize that they were saved by God's grace and not by their own works. Or were there some, perhaps many, who like some Christians today, did not grasp the foundational reality of grace, but kept attempting to justify themselves before God through their deeds? If there were, then the traditional understanding of Paul's polemic against the Law makes sense in the first century, even as it does today.

The New Perspective on Paul seems to be part of an increasingly popular pattern of understanding the NT and early Christianity in as fully Jewish terms as possible. Thus Jesus is understood as a Jewish charismatic healer-teacher, who fits comfortably among other figures in first-century Palestine. Paul is an unexceptional Jew, with no disagreement with Judaism or the Law, except for his desire to include the Gentiles as also the subjects of God's grace. The Gospel of Matthew is to be understood as a Christian Judaism rather than a Jewish Christianity. Many now think that it is improper to speak of "Christianity" until sometime in the middle of the second century. Hence, in the first century—and thus through the whole of the NT period— it is improper to speak of "Jewish Christians," but only of "Jewish believers in Jesus." Indeed, it is even improper to speak of Gentiles as "Christians." What we have traditionally called "Christianity" in the first century, and even later, is now regarded as a "sect" of Judaism, like other sects, such as the Essenes or the Pharisees.

There is much that is good and helpful about this new realization of the Jewish character of the Christian faith. But this insight can also cause distortion. In fact it totally neglects or underestimates the dramatic newness that is intrinsic to Jesus and the faith of his followers. A correct understanding of that faith comes only through an appreciation of both the old and the new. The Evangelist Matthew records Jesus as making the point in these words: "Therefore every scribe who has been trained for the kingdom of heaven is like a householder who brings out of his treasure what is new [*kaina*] and what is old [*palaia*]" (Matt 13:52), even placing priority upon the new by mentioning it before the old. But the revisionist readings of the NT that have become fashionable in recent years are so fascinated with Christianity's roots in the old that they pay little or no attention to the new. There is far more newness in the gospel according to Paul than simply the inclusion of the Gentiles.

One of the most commonly heard criticisms of the traditional understanding of Paul is that it reads Paul through Lutheran eyes. Luther was plagued with the question of how he could become acceptable to God. Paul, a good Jew and hence a participant in God's covenant with Israel, had no such problem. At least, if Paul did have such a problem, it assumed nowhere near the significance it had for Luther. Sanders may well be right that Paul began to see the enormity of the human predicament only when he began to trace out the rationale that had required the death of the Messiah. The problem of sin, the central human problem, assumed new proportions corresponding to the remedy of the death of the Son of God.

There can be no question, however, that Paul, after the risen Christ appeared to him on the Damascus Road, drew a bold contrast between his former preoccupation with "a righteousness of my own, based on law [*ek nomou*]," and the new reality of a righteousness "which is through faith in Christ, the righteousness from God [*ek theou*] that depends on faith" (Phil 3:9). The former he now rejects as a cul-de-sac; the latter alone is of any consequence. But if Paul had earlier appealed to a righteousness based on the Law, there were probably many in his day who would have done the same.

The New Perspective raises new questions and new possibilities that should never be abruptly dismissed. As Yinger stresses, it is always worthwhile to re-examine the Pauline texts, and to consider whether we have understood Paul correctly. We must always remain open to refining our conclusions as it becomes necessary.

I personally do not think that it is necessary to reject the traditional understanding of Paul even though we may find from the New Perspective that we need to nuance our statements about Paul to some extent. I want finally to stress two fixed points—i.e., what appear to me to be non-negotiables, not because I have predetermined them, but because I think they are so rooted in the Pauline texts.

First, salvation is the work of God, and solely the work of God. The Bible is the story of God consistently taking the initiative to save us. This is the very essence of grace. And it is the consistent emphasis straight through the OT and NT. Salvation is ultimately dependent upon the cross of Christ, even for the people of the OT. The atoning death of the Savior is the ground of salvation, and all who experience salvation can do so only because of the cross. This means furthermore that there is only one way of salvation for both Jews and Gentiles. And it is for this reason that the gospel must go to the Jews first and only then to the Gentiles.

Second, the righteousness of the believer is a requirement for salvation. Practical, or lived-out, righteousness is necessary but it is not the grounds, basis, or cause of justi-fication. As Dr. Yinger's earlier work shows, a judgment of works faces all human beings. Righteousness is not optional for the Christian. But do we not then have a synergism wherein salvation is the result of the cooperation of God and human beings? As logical as such a conclusion may sound, it simply goes against the whole drift of the biblical texts, which constantly point to God alone as the one who saves, indeed as one who saves the sinner. The difference is that the righteousness of the believer follows and does not precede salvation. And the sanctification of the believer too is the gift of God, also a matter of grace. For paradoxically, it is only by power of the Holy Spirit that Christians are enabled to live righteously. Christ died, says Paul, "in order that the just requirement of the law might be fulfilled in us, who walk not according to the flesh but according to the Spirit" (Rom 8:4). The believer's practice of righteousness, by the way, was also a very deep concern for Luther—next to Paul, the boldest champion of salvation by faith alone.

Dr. Yinger will not disagree with my main points. And to the extent that they are acceptable to other reasonable advocates of the New Perspective, we may perhaps see the New Perspective as offering friendly adjustments, some right, some perhaps wrong, to our understanding of specific Pauline texts. In the end may it be that our appreciation of the gospel and our love for God will increase and abound to his glory.

Donald A. Hagner
George Eldon Ladd Professor Emeritus of New Testament
Fuller Theological Seminary

AFTERWORD
BY DON GARLINGTON

PROFESSOR KENT Yinger has favored us with the finest introduction to the New Perspective on Paul (NPP) to date. Within the scope of relatively few pages, he has outlined the arguments pro and con in a fair and balanced manner and in a style that makes for easy reading for the non-specialist in the field. In brief, I would like to address several of the sticking points posed by the NPP debate as taken up in this book.

For one, there is the hermeneutically important issue of the historical setting of the New Testament generally and of Paul's letters in particular. We should recall that the phrase "New Perspective" was coined by J. D. G. Dunn in his Manson Memorial Lecture of 1982. Dunn's original point had to do with Paul's relation to Second Temple Judaism, with special reference to the phrase "the works of the law." To be sure, Dunn's position has been refined and qualified over the years, both by himself and others. Nevertheless, the NPP has sought to understand the New Testament in such a way that balances text and context. Certainly, it is the text that receives the priority. But the New Testament was not written in a vacuum, and any reading of it has to be sensitive to the issues that were being debated within its own milieu, not ours. To put it bluntly, the four hundred years leading up to Paul are more important for our understanding of him than the four hundred years since the Reformation to the present day. Before we ask what the New Testament *means*, we have to ask what it *meant*. In the end, everything boils down to the interpretive task of determining both the "meaning" and the "significance" (application) of the text.

In this notable regard, the NPP represents an advance over the traditional (Lutheran/Reformational) understanding of Paul in relation to his Jewish contemporaries. It is certainly arguable that Protestant/evangelical commentators on Paul, from Luther onward, have made an appropriate application of the apostle's disputes with his compatriots. That is to say, if justification is not by Jewish tradition ("works of the law"), then it is not by church tradition either, à la Luther's famed struggle with medieval Catholicism. It is too easily forgotten that the Reformation began not with questions about justification but with Luther's Ninety-Five Theses, which challenged a dangerous and outrageous component of church tradition (indulgences), as followed up later by Luther's merciless lampooning of the collection and veneration of relics, such as splinters of "the true cross." But even given this qualification, the "legalistic" framework imposed on the Judaism of Paul's day by Luther and his theological heirs has served to muddy the waters more than anything else. When read in their own context, the central issue of Paul's polemical letters boils down to a simple choice: Christ or the Torah as the "gateway of salvation."

In the second place, subsequent to Dunn's original premise, the issue of a future dimension of justification was attached to the NPP, especially with the contributions of N. T. Wright thrown into the mix. This was bound to happen, given that much of the literature of Second Temple Judaism was engendered by the necessity of faith and perseverance in a time of persecution and of temptation to forsake Israel's national heritage. The sum of the matter is stated in 1 Maccabees 1:15: many in Israel "abandoned the holy covenant." It is against this backdrop that NPP scholars have understood Pauline phrases such as "the obedience of faith" (Rom 1:5; 16:26). Simply stated, if Jews were expected to maintain faith in God by observing his Law, Christians are expected to remain faithful to Christ by doing his will; their covenant fidelity will eventuate in eschatological salvation.

While this theology of the "perseverance of the saints" is hardly new, the NPP has sought to take the New Testament materials seriously by stressing that there is a phase of the vindication of God's people that is yet to be. Like most aspects of soteriology, justification too takes on an "already" and a "not yet" aspect. In a nutshell, phase one of justification is by faith alone, and phase two is by a faith that works. When viewed in such a manner, Paul's insistence that the doers of the Law (not the hearers only) will be justified (Rom 2:13) places him on "the same page" with James, not only James 2:14–26 but the entire letter. The fear of many is that such an understanding of Paul results in "contributing to salvation" by means of "synergism." Yet the fear is unfounded, simply because of the nature of a biblical covenant.

In other words, once God enters into a bond with a human partner, faithfulness is required of both parties, and the NPP has endeavored to underscore what the biblical text itself repeatedly emphasizes. Outside of Paul, the root of the matter is voiced by James (1:21): "Therefore put away all filthiness and rank growth of wickedness and receive with meekness the implanted word, which is able to save your souls." Likewise, the risen Christ encourages the persecuted church at Smyrna with these words: "Be faithful unto death, and I will give you the crown of life" (Rev 2:10).

Third, there is Paul's theology of union with Christ. From the non-NPP side, much is made of the imputation of Christ's righteousness and the "basis" of justification. To cut to the chase, NPP scholars of the evangelical stripe gladly affirm that our righteousness comes from Christ. It is not this basic premise that is in dispute, but rather the modality of the process. Speaking for myself only, in Paul's letters there is abundant evidence of union with Christ but none for the traditional doctrine of imputation. Such being the case, my own brand of the NPP places its emphasis on the relational aspect of believers with the savior, who are "in Christ," all the while mindful of the forensic component of that relationship. As regards Paul's basic message to Israel in particular, the people of God are no longer identified as those who are "in the law" and "of the law." Rather, in the place of the Law he has substituted a person, a person who has rendered the Law obsolete by demolishing "the dividing wall of hostility" that once so radically bifurcated the Jewish and Gentile members of the human race (Eph 2:14–15). As for the "basis" of justification, it is simply a fact that Paul does not characteristically use such language (the only possible instance is Phil 3:9: "the righteousness that depends on [*epi*] faith"). Instead, he uses prepositions of origin, sphere, and location (principally *en* and *ek*). At heart, the issue is simple: what counts now and in the judgment is being *en Christō*. To press for a "basis" of justification is another case where theological jargon has clouded rather than clarified the Pauline teaching.

Apart from the "basis of justification" discussion, each of the "sticking points" (and numerous other points) is so helpfully addressed by Professor Yinger's book, especially as his approach is eminently exegetical rather than "ecclesiastical." Because the NPP is closer to variations on a theme than a monolithic entity, assessments of this volume will differ according to individual readers. As a proponent of the "Sanders/Dunn trajectory" (Moisés Silva), I would have argued more vigorously for my version of the NPP. Yet one of the decided strengths of this introductory volume is just its balance and its willingness to let readers decide for themselves. The irenic attitude of the book is all the more appropriate since, among believers, it is imperative always to exhibit the Beroean spirit of searching the Scriptures to see "if these things are so" (Acts 17:11). And it is my hope that this book will be used to that end as the conversation continues.

Don Garlington
Toronto, Ontario

WORKS CITED

Abbreviations used in Works Cited and Suggestions for Further Study:

JSNTSup   Journal for the Study of the New Testament Supplement
NICNT   New International Commentary on the New Testament
NIGTC   New International Greek Testament Commentary
SNTSMS   Society for New Testament Studies Monograph Series
WUNT   Wissenschaftliche Untersuchungen zum Neuen
          Testament

Barclay, John M. G. "Paul and the Law: Observations on Some Recent Debates." *Themelios* 12 (1986) 5–15.

Barnett, Paul. *Paul: Missionary of Jesus.* Grand Rapids: Eerdmans, 2008.

Bird, Michael F. *The Saving Righteousness of God: Studies on Paul, Justification and the New Perspective.* Paternoster Biblical Monographs. Eugene, OR: Wipf & Stock, 2007.

Braaten, Carl E., and Robert W. Jenson. *Union with Christ: The New Finnish Interpretation of Luther.* Grand Rapids: Eerdmans, 1998.

Bultmann, Rudolf Karl. *Theology of the New Testament.* Translated by Kendrick Grobel. 2 vols. London: SCM, 1952–55.

Campbell, Douglas A. *The Quest for Paul's Gospel: A Suggested Strategy.* JSNTSup 274. London: T. & T. Clark, 2005.

Carson, D. A. "The Vindication of Imputation: On Fields of Discourse and Semantic Fields." In *Justification: What's at Stake in the Current Debates?*, edited by Mark Husbands and Daniel J. Treier, 46–78. Downers Grove, IL: InterVarsity, 2004.

Carson, Donald A., Peter T. O'Brien, and Mark A. Seifrid, editors. *Justification and Variegated Nomism*. Vol. 1, *The Complexities of Second Temple Judaism*. WUNT 2/140. Grand Rapids: Baker Academic, 2001.

Comment on "Justification by Faith Alone through Grace Alone by Christ Alone and Peace with God," sermon by Charles Spurgeon. Online: http://www.sermonaudio.com/sermoninfo.asp?SID=15040458.

Cranford, Michael. "The Possibility of Perfect Obedience: Paul and an Implied Premise in Galatians 3:10 and 5:3." *Novum Testamentum* 36 (1994) 242–58.

"Critiques of NPP." Monergism.com. Online: http://www.monergism .com/directory/link_category/New-Perspective-on-Paul/General -Essays-Critiquing-NPP.

Das, A. Andrew. *Paul and the Jews*. Library of Pauline Studies. Peabody, MA: Hendrickson, 2003.

Dunn, James D. G. *Jesus, Paul, and the Law: Studies in Mark and Galatians*. Louisville: Westminster John Knox, 1990.

———. "The Justice of God: A Renewed Perspective on Justification by Faith." *Journal of Theological Studies* 43 (1992) 1–22.

———. "The Narrative Approach to Paul: Whose Story?" In *Narrative Dynamics in Paul: A Critical Assessment*, edited by Bruce W. Longenecker, 217–30. Louisville: Westminster John Knox, 2002.

———. *The New Perspective on Paul*. Rev. ed. Grand Rapids: Eerdmans, 2008.

———. "The New Perspective on Paul: Whence, What and Whither?" In *The New Perspective on Paul Revised Edition*, 1–97. Grand Rapids: Eerdmans, 2008.

———. "Philippians 3.2–14 and the New Perspective on Paul." In *The New Perspective on Paul Revised Edition*, 469–90. Grand Rapids: Eerdmans, 2008.

———. "Works of the Law and the Curse of the Law (Gal. 3.10–14)." In *Jesus, Paul, and the Law: Studies in Mark and Galatians*, 215–41. Louisville: Westminster John Knox, 1990.

————. "Yet Once More—'The Works of the Law': A Response." In *The New Perspective on Paul Revised Edition*, 213–26. Grand Rapids: Eerdmans, 2008.

Dunn, James D. G., and Alan M. Suggate, *The Justice of God: A Fresh Look at the Old Doctrine of Justification by Faith*. Grand Rapids: Eerdmans, 1994.

Fink, David C. "Was There a 'Reformation Doctrine of Justification'?" *Harvard Theological Review* 103 (2010) 205–35.

Gager, John G. *The Origins of Anti-Semitism: Attitudes toward Judaism in Pagan and Christian Antiquity*. New York: Oxford University Press, 1983.

Garlington, Don B. "Imputation or Union with Christ? A Rejoinder to John Piper." Online: http://www.thepaulpage.com/Piper_Rejoinder.pdf.

————. *In Defense of the New Perspective on Paul: Essays and Reviews*. Eugene, OR: Wipf & Stock, 2005.

————. "The New Perspective on Paul: Two Decades On." In *In Defense of the New Perspective on Paul: Essays and Reviews*, 1–28. Eugene, OR: Wipf & Stock, 2005.

————. *The Obedience of Faith: A Pauline Phrase in Historical Context*. WUNT 2/38. Tübingen: Mohr/Siebeck, 1991.

Gaston, Lloyd. *Paul and the Torah*. Vancouver: University of British Columbia Press, 1987.

Gathercole, Simon J. *Where Is Boasting?: Early Jewish Soteriology and Paul's Response in Romans 1–5*. Grand Rapids, MI: Eerdmans, 2002.

Gilley, Gary. "The New Perspective on Paul, Part 1." Online: http://www.svchapel.org/resources/articles/23-doctrine/559-the-new-perspective-on-paul-part-1.

Grundmann, W. "*Memphomai*, etc." In *Theological Dictionary of the New Testament*, edited by G. Kittel and G. Friedrich, 4:571–73. Grand Rapids: Eerdmans, 1964.

Gundry, Robert H. "The Nonimputation of Christ's Righteousness." In *Justification: What's at Stake in the Current Debates?*, edited by Mark Husbands and Daniel J. Treier, 17–45. Downers Grove, IL: InterVarsity, 2004.

Hagner, Donald A. "Paul and Judaism, the Jewish Matrix of Early Christianity: Issues in the Current Debate." *Bulletin for Biblical Research* 3 (1993) 111–30.

Hays, Richard B. *The Faith of Jesus Christ: The Narrative Substructure of Galatians 3:1—4:11*. 2nd ed. Grand Rapids: Eerdmans, 2002.

Holmgren, Fredrick C. "The Pharisee and the Tax Collector. Luke 18:9–14 and Deuteronomy 26:1–15." *Interpretation* 48 (1994) 252–61.

Hooker, Morna D. "Paul and 'Covenantal Nomism.'" In *Paul and Paulinism: Essays in Honour of C. K. Barrett*, edited by M. D. Hooker and S. G. Wilson, 47–56. London: SPCK, 1982.

Horsley, Richard A. "Introduction." In *Paul and the Imperial Order*, edited by Richard A. Horsley, 1–23. Harrisburg, PA: Trinity, 2004.

Jüngel, Eberhard. *Justification: The Heart of the Christian Faith*. Translated by Jeffrey F. Cayzer. 3rd ed. Edinburgh: T. & T. Clark, 2001.

Kedar-Kopfstein, B. "*Tamam*, etc." In *Theological Dictionary of the Old Testament*, edited by G. J. Botterweck et al., 15:699–711. Grand Rapids: Eerdmans, 2006.

Kennedy, Kevin D. *Union with Christ and the Extent of the Atonement in Calvin*. Studies in Biblical Literature 48. New York: Lang, 2002.

Kümmel, Werner Georg. *Römer 7 und das Bild des Menschen im Neuen Testament: Zwei Studien*. Theologische Bücherei 53. Munich: Kaiser, 1974.

Kwakkel, Gert. *According to My Righteousness: Upright Behaviour as Grounds for Deliverance in Psalms 7, 17, 18, 26, and 44*. Oudtestamentische Studiën 46. Leiden: Brill, 2002.

Lambrecht, Jan. *The Wretched "I" and Its Liberation: Paul in Romans 7 and 8*. Louvain Theological and Pastoral Monographs 14. Grand Rapids: Eerdmans, 1992.

Lincoln, Andrew T. "Ephesians 2:8–10: A Summary of Paul's Gospel?" *Catholic Biblical Quarterly* 45 (1983) 617–30.

Longenecker, Bruce W. "Lifelines: Perspectives on Paul and the Law." *Anvil* 16 (1999) 125–30.

———. *The Triumph of Abraham's God: The Transformation of Identity in Galatians*. Nashville: Abingdon, 1998.

Martínez, Florentíno Garcia, editor. *The Dead Sea Scrolls Translated: The Qumran Texts in English*. Translated by Wilfred G. E. Watson. 2nd ed. Grand Rapids: Eerdmans, 1996.

Mattison, Mark. "Confronting Legalism or Exclusivism? Reconsidering Key Pauline Passages." Online: http://www.thepaulpage.com/confronting-legalism-or-exclusivism-reconsidering-key-pauline-passages.

Metzger, Bruce M. *The New Testament: Its Background, Growth, and Content*. Nashville: Abingdon, 1965.

Middleton, Darren. "Pastoral Implications of the New Perspective (Part 3 of 3)." Online: http://www.thirdmill.org/files/english/html/th/TH.h.Middleton.new.perspective.3.html.

Moo, Douglas J. "Israel and Paul in Romans 7:7–12." *New Testament Studies* 32 (1986) 122–35.

Moore, George Foot. "Christian Writers on Judaism." *Harvard Theological Review* 14 (1921) 197–254.

———. *Judaism in the First Centuries of the Christian Era, The Age of the Tannaim*. 3 vols. Cambridge: Harvard University Press, 1927.

Neusner, Jacob. "Paul and Palestinian Judaism: A Comparison of Patterns of Religion." *History of Religions* 18 (1978) 177–91.

Olson, Roger E. *The Mosaic of Christian Belief: Twenty Centuries of Unity and Diversity*. Downers Grove, IL: InterVarsity, 2002.

The Paul Page. Online: http://www.thepaulpage.com.

Piper, John, *The Future of Justification: A Response to N.T. Wright*. Wheaton, IL: Crossway, 2007.

Räisänen, Heikki. *Paul and the Law*. 1st Fortress ed. Philadelphia, PA: Fortress, 1986.

Rakestraw, Robert V. "John Wesley as a Theologian of Grace." *Journal of the Evangelical Theological Society* 27 (1984) 193–203.

Reumann, John H., and Joseph A. Fitzmyer. *Righteousness in the New Testament: Justification in the United States: Lutheran–Roman Catholic Dialogue*. Philadelphia: Fortress, 1982.

Sanders, E. P. "Covenantal Nomism Revisited." *Jewish Studies Quarterly* 16 (2009) 25–55.

———. *Paul and Palestinian Judaism: A Comparison of Patterns of Religion*. Philadelphia: Fortress, 1977.

Schechter, S. *Aspects of Rabbinic Theology: Major Concepts of the Talmud*. New York: Schocken, 1961.

Schreiner, Thomas R. "Is Perfect Obedience to the Law Possible: A Re-Examination of Galatians 3:10." *Journal of the Evangelical Theological Society* 27 (1984) 151–60.

Segal, Alan F. *Paul the Convert: The Apostolate and Apostasy of Saul the Pharisee.* New Haven: Yale University Press, 1990.

Stendahl, Krister. "The Apostle Paul and the Introspective Conscience of the West." In *Paul among Jews and Gentiles and Other Essays,* 78–96. Philadelphia: Fortress, 1976.

————. *Final Account: Paul's Letter to the Romans.* Minneapolis: Fortress, 1995.

Stuhlmacher, Peter. *Revisiting Paul's Doctrine of Justification: A Challenge to the New Perspective.* Downers Grove, IL: InterVarsity, 2001.

Thompson, Michael B. *The New Perspective on Paul.* Grove Biblical Series 26. Cambridge, UK: Grove, 2002.

Trueman, Carl R. "The Portrait of Martin Luther in Contemporary New Testament Scholarship: Some Casual Observations." Lecture delivered at the Tyndale Fellowship in Christian Doctrine, 2001. Cited in "The New Perspective on Justification" by Richard D. Phillips. Online: http://www.fpcjackson.org/resources/apologetics/Modern%20Unbib%20Chall%20to%20Covt%20Theology/phillips_new_perspective.htm.

Venema, Cornelis P. *The Gospel of Free Acceptance in Christ: An Assessment of the Reformation and New Perspectives on Paul.* Edinburgh: Banner of Truth Trust, 2006.

Visscher, Gerhard H. *Romans 4 and the New Perspective on Paul: Faith Embraces the Promise.* Studies in Biblical Literature 122. New York: Lang, 2009.

Warfield, B. B. "Imputation." In *The New Schaff-Herzog Encyclopedia of Religious Knowledge,* edited by S. M. Jackson, 5:465–67. Grand Rapids: Baker, 1977.

Watson, Francis. "Not the New Perspective." An unpublished paper delivered at the British New Testament Conference, Manchester, September 2001. Online: http://www.abdn.ac.uk/divinity/staff/watsonart.shtml.

————. *Paul, Judaism, and the Gentiles: Beyond the New Perspective.* Rev. and exp. ed. Grand Rapids: Eerdmans, 2007.

————. *Paul, Judaism, and the Gentiles: A Sociological Approach.* Cambridge: Cambridge University Press, 1986.

Weedman, Gary E. "Reading Ephesians from the New Perspective on Paul." *Leaven* 1 (2006) 81–92. Online: http://www.thepaulpage.com/Weedman.pdf.

Westerholm, Stephen. *Perspectives Old and New on Paul: The "Lutheran" Paul and His Critics*. Grand Rapids: Eerdmans, 2004.

Wright, N. T. *The Climax of the Covenant: Christ and the Law in Pauline Theology*. Minneapolis: Fortress, 1993.

———. *Justification: God's Plan and Paul's Vision*. Downers Grove, IL: InterVarsity Academic, 2009.

———. "The Letter to the Romans." In *The New Interpreter's Bible*. Vol. 10, *Acts, Introduction to Epistolary Literature, Romans, 1 Corinthians*, edited by Leander E. Keck, 393–770. Nashville: Abingdon, 2002.

———. "New Perspectives on Paul." Online: http://www.ntwright-page.com/Wright_New_Perspectives.htm.

———. *Paul for Everyone: Romans*. Louisville: Westminster John Knox, 2004.

———. *Paul: In Fresh Perspective*. Minneapolis: Fortress, 2005.

———. "The Paul of History and the Apostle of Faith." *Tyndale Bulletin* 29 (1978) 61–88.

———. "Redemption from the New Perspective? Towards a Multi-Layered Pauline Theology of the Cross." In *Redemption*, edited by S. T. Davis, D. Kendall, and G. O'Collins, 69–100. Oxford: Oxford University Press, 2006. Online: http://www.ntwrightpage.com/Wright_Redemption_NPP.htm.

———. *What Saint Paul Really Said: Was Paul of Tarsus the Real Founder of Christianity?* Grand Rapids: Eerdmans, 1997.

Yinger, Kent L. "The Continuing Quest for Jewish Legalism." *Bulletin of Biblical Research* 19 (2009) 375–91.

———. "Defining 'Legalism.'" *Andrews University Seminary Studies* 46 (2008) 91–108.

———. *Paul, Judaism, and Judgment According to Deeds*. SNTSMS 105. Cambridge: Cambridge University Press, 1999.

———. "Reformation Redivivus: Synergism and the New Perspective." *Journal for Theological Interpretation* 3 (2009) 89–106.

Zahl, Paul F. M. "Mistakes of the New Perspective on Paul." *Themelios* 27 (2001) 5–11.

SUGGESTIONS FOR
FURTHER STUDY
(ANNOTATED)

OVERVIEWS AND INTRODUCTIONS

The Paul Page. Online: http://www.thepaulpage.com. Large collection
of full-text NPP-related writings; continually updated.

Thompson, Michael B. *The New Perspective on Paul*. Grove Biblical
Series 26. Cambridge, UK: Grove, 2002. Brief and readable, but
hard to obtain in the US.

SANDERS AND A NEW
PERSPECTIVE ON JUDAISM

Carson, Donald A., Peter T. O'Brien, and Mark A. Seifrid, editors.
Justification and Variegated Nomism. Vol. 1, *The Complexities of
Second Temple Judaism*. WUNT 2/140. Grand Rapids: Baker Academic, 2001. Examines a broad range of Second Temple literature
to determine if covenantal nomism was characteristic.

Gathercole, Simon J. *Where Is Boasting?: Early Jewish Soteriology and
Paul's Response in Romans 1–5*. Grand Rapids: Eerdmans, 2002.
Jewish soteriology was at least synergistic (both divine grace
and human obedience), if not legalistic; Paul, on the other hand,
preached "by grace alone."

Moore, George Foot. "Christian Writers on Judaism." *Harvard Theological Review* 14 (1921) 197–254. An important pre-Sanders protest against Christian portrayals of Judaism.

Sanders, E. P. "Covenantal Nomism Revisited." *Jewish Studies Quarterly* 16 (2009) 25–55. Sanders holds firm against critics after 30+ years of challenges.

———. *Paul and Palestinian Judaism: A Comparison of Patterns of Religion*. Philadelphia: Fortress, 1977, esp. pp. 33–428. This book forced a re-evaluation of the type of Judaism to which Paul might be responding.

———. *Judaism: Practice and Belief, 63 BCE–66 CE*. Philadelphia: Trinity, 1992. Explores how the large majority of common Jews (non-Pharisees, non-Sadducees, etc.) would have lived and believed as covenantal nomists.

Yinger, Kent L. "The Continuing Quest for Jewish Legalism." *Bulletin of Biblical Research* 19 (2009) 375–91. Surveys post-Sanders study of Jewish soteriology.

FAVORING THE NEW PERSPECTIVE ON PAUL

Dunn, James D. G. *The New Perspective on Paul*. Rev. ed. Grand Rapids: Eerdmans, 2008. Reprints of Dunn's influential essays, including the initial call for such a "new perspective." Includes some new articles and updates of older ones.

Dunn, James D. G., and Alan M. Suggate, *The Justice of God: A Fresh Look at the Old Doctrine of Justification by Faith*. Grand Rapids: Eerdmans, 1994. Dunn and Suggate respond to charges that the NPP abandons justification by faith alone.

Garlington, Don B. *In Defense of the New Perspective on Paul: Essays and Reviews*. Eugene, OR: Wipf & Stock, 2005. Helpful responses to numerous criticisms of the NPP and reviews of a number of critical books.

Stendahl, Krister. "The Apostle Paul and the Introspective Conscience of the West." In *Paul among Jews and Gentiles*, 78–96. Philadelphia: Fortress, 1976. Although pre-dating the NPP, this essay has proven highly influential for most NPP writers.

Wright, N. T. "The Paul of History and the Apostle of Faith." *Tyndale Bulletin* 29 (1978) 61–88. One of the earliest expressions of the NPP.

————. *The Climax of the Covenant: Christ and the Law in Pauline Theology*. Minneapolis: Fortress, 1993. Important essays showing Wright's NPP.

————. *Paul: In Fresh Perspective*. Minneapolis: Fortress, 2005. A non-academic update of Wright's position. Moves beyond the "new" to a "fresh" perspective which includes imperial aspects.

————. *What Saint Paul Really Said: Was Paul of Tarsus the Real Founder of Christianity?* Grand Rapids: Eerdmans, 1997. Originally lectures on various NPP-related topics (justification, conversion, etc.).

————. Online: http://www.ntwrightpage.com. Many of N. T. Wright's publications, lectures, and unpublished papers are accessible here.

Yinger, Kent L. *Paul, Judaism, and Judgment according to Deeds*. SNTSMS 105. Cambridge: Cambridge University Press, 1999. Explores Paul's use of the Jewish motif "judgment according to deeds."

CRITICAL OF THE NEW PERSPECTIVE ON PAUL

Carson, D. A., Peter Thomas O'Brien, and Mark A. Seifrid. *Justification and Variegated Nomism*. Vol. 2, *The Paradoxes of Paul*. WUNT 2/140. Grand Rapids: Baker Academic, 2004. Sustained academic critique of NPP interpretations.

Hagner, Donald A. "Paul and Judaism, the Jewish Matrix of Early Christianity: Issues in the Current Debate." *Bulletin for Biblical Research* 3 (1993) 111–30. A balanced and readable presentation of criticisms.

Venema, Cornelis P. *The Gospel of Free Acceptance in Christ: An Assessment of the Reformation and New Perspectives on Paul*. Edinburgh: Banner of Truth Trust, 2006. Argues that the NPP and the Reformation are theologically incompatible.

Waters, Guy Prentiss. *Justification and the New Perspectives on Paul: A Review and Response*. Phillipsburg, NJ: P&R, 2004. An energetic Reformed critique of the NPP.

Westerholm, Stephen. *Perspectives Old and New on Paul: The "Lutheran" Paul and His Critics*. Grand Rapids: Eerdmans, 2004. Probably the best academic overview and critique to-date.

FROM THE MANY WEB SITES CRITICAL OF THE NEW PERSPECTIVE ON PAUL

"Critiques of NPP." Monergism.com. Online: http://www.monergism .com/directory/link_category/New-Perspective-on-Paul/General-Essays-Critiquing-NPP.

"The New Perspective." First Presbyterian Church of Jackson Mississippi. Online: http://www.fpcjackson.org/resources/apologetics/ Modern%20Unbib%20Chall%20to%20Covt%20Theology/modern_unbibl_challeng_%20index.htm#The%20New%20Perspective.

PROPOSING A "BOTH/AND" OR "BEYOND" POSITION ON THE NPP

Bird, Michael F. *The Saving Righteousness of God: Studies on Paul, Justification and the New Perspective*. Paternoster Biblical Monographs. Eugene, OR: Wipf & Stock, 2007. Favors "incorporated righteousness" over "imputed."

Campbell, Douglas A. *The Quest for Paul's Gospel: A Suggested Strategy*. JSNTSup 274. London: T. & T. Clark, 2005. Favors apocalyptic categories; finds some value in the NPP and strongly critiques a Lutheran approach.

Das, A. Andrew. *Paul and the Jews*. Library of Pauline Studies. Peabody, MA : Hendrickson, 2003. Sanders was correct about Judaism, but Paul was still opposing legalism.

Longenecker, Bruce W. *The Triumph of Abraham's God: The Transformation of Identity in Galatians*. Nashville: Abingdon, 1998. Academic study of Galatians from a "complementarity" perspective (i.e., NPP and non-NPP positions complement one another).

———. "Lifelines: Perspectives on Paul and the Law." *Anvil* 16 (1999) 125–30. Brief and non-academic presentation of Longenecker's "complementarity" position (see previous entry).

Watson, Francis. *Paul, Judaism, and the Gentiles: Beyond the New Perspective*. Rev. and exp. ed. Grand Rapids: Eerdmans, 2007. Watson explains his dissatisfaction with both traditional and NPP approaches to Paul.

SUBJECT INDEX